FROM SICK & TIRED TO BACK ON FIRE:

How High-Performing Men Over 40 Can Stop the Slide, Recapture Their Youth, and Become Unstoppable Again

LOGAN HENRY

FROM SICK & TIRED TO BACK ON FIRE™

How High-Performing Men Over 40 Can Stop the Slide, Recapture Their Youth, and Become Unstoppable Again

Design and cover art by Jahz Rivera.

Disclaimer: The author makes no guarantees to the results you'll achieve by reading this book. Sudden health and wellness changes may pose a physical risk or injury. The information contained in this book is for informational purposes only and is not intended as a substitute for professional medical advice, diagnosis, or treatment. The author shall not be held liable for any direct, indirect, incidental, or consequential damages arising out of the use or inability to use the information contained in this book. The results and client case studies presented in this book represent results achieved by fully committing to their own personalized program, putting in the effort, and working directly with the author. Your results may vary when undertaking any new health or wellness improvement plan. By reading this book, you acknowledge and accept that the author is not responsible for any adverse effects or consequences resulting from the use of any information contained in this book. It is important to consult with your primary care physician before making any dramatic changes to diet, supplementation, and engaging in any kind of new physical activity.

“

To my loving wife, Erica, and to my first mentor, Greg, who inspired me to make a change and become a better man. And to my future son, (he is “on the way”, as they say, due in a few months as this book went to press), who will bring endless joy and meaning to my life and inspire me to be the best version of myself, every day.

To get the most out of this book, I've included a heap of bonuses, including:

Bonus #1:

From Sick & Tired to Back On Fire Audiobook

Bonus #2:

"The Winner's Lifestyle - How High Performers Achieve What They Want in Health, Wealth, And Life" (Mini-Course)

Bonus #3:

"Get Your Head In The Game - Clear Out The Mental Clutter and Amplify Your Productivity" (Workshop)

Please visit
https://www.backonfirebook.com/bonuses
to receive them all.

CONTENT

INTRODUCTION

I hated the guy looking back at me in the mirror.

But day after day, I was forced to see him.

He looked terrible. He had bags under his eyes and his face, (scowling more often than not), was puffy. The stress and pressure he was feeling was outwardly noticeable. The extra weight he was carrying was a constant frustration.

How had I turned into this guy? I didn't even recognize him!

How had I let it get this far?

It all seemed to happen so *quickly...*

Looking back now, I can see the hard truth: I was so consumed by life and responsibilities that I had burned myself out and had stopped paying attention to my needs and health, slowly morphing into this unrecognizable, miserable man.

Ouch.

I kept saying I'd fix it, but I was too tired. I lacked motivation. I had nowhere on my calendar to squeeze in a trip to the gym, (and even if I had, I'd surely only make it as far as the parking lot for a quick nap).

To make things worse, I felt selfish every time I tried to do something about it...

My thinking was, "What gives me the right to make *myself* feel better? I'm supposed to take care of everyone else, aren't I?"

I was put here to provide for my family. I'm supposed to lead my team.

I was NOT in a good space. I'll spare you the ugly details, but suffice it to say that I finally realized I HAD to change.

I *had* to make a choice.

I *had* to commit to a better life.

And guess what?

I did just that...

After a ton of research, and a lot of trial and error, I discovered a long-term, *sustainable* solution that transformed my life forever.

And that's exactly what I'll be sharing with you in this book.

So if you're a man reading this right now, who's currently experiencing anything similar in your life, I encourage you to devour every word in this book as if your best life depended on it.

(Because it very well does, if I may be so bold to say.)

You too can make the change.

This is not theory. This is coming from 100 percent personal experience.

I am going to be upfront and straight with you in the pages of this short book. I'll not only share my own health journey with you but also the raw, unfiltered journeys of men who — just like you — transformed their lives in ways they never imagined. (And all of it happening a lot faster than they thought it would. Wait till you hear their stories.)

The methods I teach are firmly rooted in a philosophy that redefines what "healthy" means. I'll be busting plenty of myths along the way. For example, forget about going all "beast-mode" at the gym and eating rabbit food.

The good news is - this is way easier and more delicious than you would ever expect.

HOW TO READ THIS BOOK

This book exists for 3 reasons:

Reason #1: To hit you between the eyes with the cost of inaction

Look, your health *matters*. A LOT. Your entire life depends on it ... literally! If you do nothing, things will just get worse. So this book is partly a wakeup call. And also a kick in the ass to get you headed in the right direction back to good health and deep fulfillment in all areas of your life.

Reason #2: To debunk the "hustle & grind" myth put forth by so-called health "pros"

Real talk: There's a LOT of bad information out there. I'm here to save you time and money. For example, there's a reason that grinding away on the elliptical every day at the gym, or at home on the Peleton, might not be giving you the results you want. You'll find out why in the pages of this book. And I'll give you a clear, concise plan of action that gets real results instead.

Reason #3: To recapture your lost energy, kickstart your health journey, and register some quick wins

I know that if you get real value — and most importantly,

real results — from this short book, then you'll eventually consider working with me for even more significant, long-term results that reverberate throughout your entire life.

Look, I'm fully aware that you may have tried it all: all the diets, workout programs, personal trainers, supplements, etc. I know there's a part of you that wants to believe this will work, but I also wouldn't blame you for wondering:

"But how could it when nothing else has stuck?"

Well, I have two answers to that:

Number one, you won't have to take my word for it. You're about to see the stories of others who have proven that what I have to say flat-out works. 'Nuff said.

And number two, by the time you finish this book, you're going to know exactly HOW and WHY my program works. You'll know this because I'm going to spell it out for you and blow your mind with some startling information.

And make no mistake. It's true what they say: *Information is power.* You'll soon understand every roadblock you're experiencing right now, along with how to fix it. It starts with crucial information you're about to discover.

Fact is, you've been missing key information this whole time. Information the "gurus" and "pros" ignore to keep you in a cycle of striving instead of consistently hitting your goals.

(Rather than help you get results quickly and make sure those results stick, they keep dragging you along with false hope that if you "keep at it," one day you'll be able to finally hit your goals. Except that "finally" never happens. *Oof.*)

No matter your current situation, this book was carefully put together with you in mind. For instance, you'll have the opportunity to personally assess where you are within each of the problem areas to get an accurate picture of where you are starting from.

Consider this book as your sign to turn around and reset.

It all comes down to a simple choice and your willingness to ask yourself this one question:

"How much longer am I willing to tolerate where I'm at right now?"

I encourage you to answer this honestly.

You're a smart guy, and I know that you know you've got people in your life who not only depend on you...

They also want to see you around for the long haul.

Don't let them down.

Don't let YOU down.

I promise that if you follow the methods in this book, you will start to maximize your energy, regain your edge, and take back control of your health so you can feel like you're 25 again, ready to rip the door off the hinges.

The information you're about to read is what allowed me to completely recalibrate my life for the better.

But this is not about me. The men you're about to meet in this book have also used these strategies to dramatically improve their lives, (often to their shock and amazement).

They wake up refreshed and ready to tackle the day. Their energy has been restored, and they feel more productive than they have in years. No more sleeping away their weekends or feeling the dreaded Sunday night blues. They no longer drag through their workday, and they still feel energized and ready to engage with their families even after the longest days.

They also fit back into their favorite, sharp-looking clothes again. They feel comfortable taking off their shirt on vacation and walking tall with a newfound inner confidence and power.

Believe me, life is sooooo much better when you feel and look this great!

My mission is to reconnect men with the guy they remember being and the guy they want to be again — only better.

I hope this book inspires you to get started on your own health journey. If you are "sick and tired of being sick and tired," then I firmly believe this book is the best way to change that.

And hey, if you're ready to fast-track this process and get some customized support for even quicker results, then please book a call with me or one of my team members here: *https://www.acceleratedmethod.com/call*

Regardless, I want you to know that helping you radically transform your health and wellness is my top priority.

By the end of this book, you'll be armed with all the proven principles, tools, and strategies to go "from sick and tired to back on fire."

I've done it myself, and I know what it takes.

Now it's your turn. Let's do this! Let's get you back on fire!

In Your Corner,

LOGAN HENRY

PART 1

Stoking the Fire: Let's Get Real About Your Health

CHAPTER 1

Two Core Principles To Reignite the Better You

Take another look at the first paragraphs of this book.

Here, let me save you the trouble of scrolling up to find it … Here again are the opening lines of my Introduction in all their copy-and-pasted glory:

I hated the guy looking back at me in the mirror.

But day after day, I was forced to see him.

He looked terrible. He had bags under his eyes and his face, (scowling more often than not), was puffy. The stress and pressure he was feeling was outwardly noticeable. The extra weight he was carrying was a constant frustration.

How had I turned into this guy? I didn't even recognize him!

How had I let it get this far?

It all seemed to happen so quickly...

Looking back now, I can see the hard truth: I was so consumed by life and responsibilities

> *that I had burned myself out and had stopped paying attention to my needs and health, slowly morphing into this unrecognizable, miserable man.*
>
> *Ouch.*

If you can relate to any of that, then ask yourself: What would it feel like to wake up with a smile because who was staring back at you in the mirror looked — *and felt!* — so good?

Instead of groaning and calculating how many hours you have left until a nap, you're energized.

Hunched shoulders and a rounded middle have given way to a pleasant physique. Not chiseled, sure, but fit. Healthy. The guy staring back at you in the mirror radiates the confidence of your 25-year-old self.

The extra pounds are gone.

The hopeless pressures and frustrations are now simply challenges worthy of your time and energy. You're so on top of the world, you may even shamelessly give your reflection the good ol' finger guns of approval.

And you accomplished it all in less than 30 minutes a day without starving yourself or grinding away at the gym.

This was my journey. And that's what I'm here to help you do.

I have helped hundreds of high-performing men achieve results — men just like you. Successful, driven, dedicated men who reached a point of complete depletion and, valiantly, continued pushing themselves forward, careening down a one-way path headed straight for burnout. They knew they needed to make a change, but they didn't have the time or energy to figure out what to do first.

It's not only possible to make this change — it's *needed.* You have too much to bring to this world, this life of yours, to stay a slave to your low energy and random cravings until the inevitable health/relationship/career crisis comes.

And it does come.

The fact that you're reading this book right now at this perfect, precise moment in your life is a turning point. It means you've not only realized where you're headed, but that you're willing to take action to reset your life; to regain your edge.

So congratulations on that. Seriously. Most guys don't even face this, let alone DO something about it! You've already proven to me that you're the type to not accept mediocrity. So much respect for that.

Anyway, I use two core principles to get your mind and body back to how they used to be:

Principle #1: Start Where You Are.

Almost all "health" methods ignore the fact that you currently have no energy and little motivation. Think about how illogical that is! If you're starting from "depleted," nothing you sign up for will work unless we get your gauges from red to green.

It would be like trying to drive your car down the street without any gas in the tank. Just ain't gonna happen.

So getting you into the green is what this book's about.

However... I want to stop here for a second.

I see you. You've gotten where you are by pushing yourself. By climbing higher and higher on the career ladder. You've set goals and completely obliterated them in the most impressive ways. And not for the glory, (or maybe a tiny bit for the glory), but because *that's just who you are.*

I'm here to tell you that your normal method of pushing through is not going to get you out of this health-hole. The gung-ho, slash-everything-and-go-bananas-for-3-weeks method will only get you short-term results. Because inevitably, you will fall off the wagon, gain back your weight, and feel worse than you did before starting.

Forcing yourself to push through intense health programs, (that aren't even designed to help you out in the long-term), is the reason you feel stuck in a constant loop of starting and stopping health programs.

What's different about my approach is: I meet you where you are, and we focus, first and foremost, on ***getting your energy back.***

Which makes it easier to implement core principle number two...

Principle #2: Sustainability.

The key to long-term health and wellness is to not hate the process. The goal is to find a method that works for you and seamlessly fits into your lifestyle. You want something easily repeatable 24/7/365.

I'll get further into what sustainable practices I recommend throughout this book.

What I'll be teaching you here are the basics of a special private coaching program I use with my clients. It's called The Accelerated Method, and it works incredibly well. Why? Because it takes into account so many factors that others miss.

This means you will:

- Prioritize your health and mental focus by showing up for yourself every single day.
- Focus on revitalizing your energy levels, no matter what's going on in your life or how busy you get.
- Eat nutritious and satisfying meals you actually enjoy that will also fuel and nourish your body and mind.
- Sleep better than you have in years. You'll wake up fully recharged (without hitting the snooze button).
- Feel more present and calm- better prepared to navigate life's stressors.
- Have a structured plan to follow so your body and mind perform at their best.

- Put yourself back in balance and feel in control. So you'll no longer feel like you're losing your grip on life.

The Accelerated Method is not a system that will fail you if you put in the effort.

If that sounds like a tall order, don't take it from me. My experience could be a fluke; (it's not.)

Take it from a few of my clients:

CASE STUDY

Hunter W., South Carolina, Business Owner

"Fat Like Daddy" — One Man's Wake-Up Call

"When I first started, I was in bad shape. I was not taking care of myself. I was depressed, sad, and just angry — all the time.

There was a constant saying around my house from my wife that *"they were sacrificed for the business."*

The real kicker was one night, I was talking with my daughter before bed, and she was talking about someone and she said, *"Yeah, they're fat, just like Daddy."* And I remember walking out of the room thinking, "Holy cow, this is bad."

However, as I went through (The Accelerated Method), things changed, and things changed quickly. I mean quicker than I would have ever thought. I started at 240 pounds, and I'm currently at 198 pounds.

My energy changed. My mindset changed. The energy I had at home with the kids changed. The energy I had to give to my business changed. My work ethic changed.

Everything changed for the better.

It was like I was almost a new person. It was immeasurable, and that happened mentally too. I didn't so much originally count on that. It got me in a better mood. It got the juices flowing, so to speak.

I was there for my family more. I was able to play with the kids more, spend more time with them, and actually keep up with them.

As I went through the program, I was given the tools to attack and handle the things that were causing the stress. Learning some of the skills and the things the program has taught me has helped me realize that I have to put myself first. Once I put myself first, I get myself in the right state of mind. Whether it be mindset, business, relationships, or nutrition and health — when I get those in place, I have a thousand times more to give to everything else.

It's just amazing how much more energy, time, effort, and knowledge I can give to the rest of the other areas of my life. I have no limits now."

— Hunter W., South Carolina, Business Owner

CASE STUDY

Ben C., Nevada, High-Performing Attorney

"My confidence levels are hugely different. My energy is much, much more leveled out. It's been tremendous."

"Before I started, I was pre-diabetic, my blood levels were up there, and I just felt like, "I need to get control of my life. I need to make some changes."

I was tipping the scales around 254. My energy levels were terrible. Around 2 or 3 o'clock, I would just have this crash where I would tell my wife, "There's got to be something wrong with me. I am exhausted."

It's hard to describe the feeling. It felt like I was just literally going to fall asleep. I was just *that* tired. Like I can't do anything else. And that was almost a daily thing. And something that was a significant hindrance because it was like every day at the same time.

I had actually even seen a doctor for it. I had been experiencing this for about a year and a half. Just really, super low energy. I almost resigned myself to the fact that maybe it's just because I'm over 40, and that's the way it's going to be for the rest of my life.

I knew I needed to change. I wasn't feeling good. All my clothes were super tight — my shirts, my suits, my bursting buttons. I was either going to have to have all my suits tailored or I had to figure something out.

So I felt pretty desperate. But also just frustrated from the lack of confidence because I'm looking at myself in the mirror every morning just hating the person that I'm seeing. I was just ashamed, upset, angry, and I felt worthless.

I've talked to you a lot about creating "Ben 2.0," just shattering the mold of the prior "old" Ben and creating a new one. I'm getting up in the morning; I'm ready to put the day in a headlock that starts immediately.

I would say that my number one, most important, and most valuable transformation has been the mental part of it. Recognizing that I can do this and that it's a choice that makes me happy. It's a choice that brings positivity in my life. It's a choice that brings energy in my life.

As far as the physical changes, I'm down from 254 pounds to 222 pounds. So I'm down 32 pounds in 90 days. My waist size has gone down from a 40 to at least a 38, and I really believe I'm ready to wear a 36. I've gone down three belt loops. I started off as an XXL. I've been in XXL for the last 20 years. Now, I'm into an XL, and I really think that I could pull off a Large.

My confidence levels are hugely different. My energy is much, much more leveled out. It's been tremendous. I'm able to go home, play with my kids.

Also, in work, I feel like I'm able to put in a consistent full day's effort, and I've seen the productivity gains from that. My productivity has been as high as it's ever been. I'm much more patient, more understanding, and not as stressed out so much. I think that just being more present has helped all of my relationships. I'm grateful that it's changed my life."

— Ben C.,Nevada, High-Performing Attorney

CASE STUDY

Rashid S., Florida, Physician

"I'm now more productive than I literally have ever been in my life."

Introduction: Rashid first signed up because of his:

- Lack of energy to get through the day
- Overall unhealthy lifestyle
- Limited drive to get a new business going

Rashid had numerous opportunities showing up in his life, but he didn't have the initial energy to pursue them. He was already drained and feeling a total lack of productivity.

Simultaneously, he was noticing that he was losing some financial opportunities presented to him.

How could he navigate new business opportunities, manage his already busy schedule, and show up for his family?

Rashid started the 12-week Accelerated Method and very quickly noticed that it was making an impact on him.

"I feel healthier, definitely more energetic in the morning, and then when I'm done with my day, and I'm at home, I'm not dead. I don't have the 3 o'clock lull.

I have things that I want to accomplish, and not only are they now done, but I can give quality time to other things that I enjoy, especially my family.

I'm now more productive than I literally have ever been in my life. I was blessed that some business opportunities came to the foreground when I started this, not that they hadn't before, but before when I tried to pursue them they decided to go a different direction. I can only attribute it to my energy and my attitude adjustment.

So I was able to expand the business, and it's just from the way I present myself and the energy that I'm exuding, which I knew was always in me because I used to have it. This has brought it back to the forefront and given me the ability to keep it going."

— Rashid S., Florida, Physician

CASE STUDY

Chris A., Texas, Business Owner

"It's just a night and day change from where I was."

Introduction: Chris's story is like so many other men who come to me looking to revamp their life and wellness. That is, he's a non-stop, on-the-go, busy business owner, and his days were spent pushing himself and navigating challenging situations, often with his temper flaring up along the way.

He was edgy, exhausted, and rapidly burning himself out.

By the end of most days, Chris was wrecked. He didn't have the energy or mental clarity left to spend quality time with his wife.

The snowball effect was quickly impacting him.

Then he went through The Accelerated Method program. After 12 weeks, he reported this:

"I'm accomplishing more, and I have more energy.

I have a happier outlook on life. I'm not reacting and flying off the handle multiple times a day. I'm able to take a breath and look at situations and form a mature, positive response, in most cases.

I mean, literally, before, it took me a lot just to get through a day without snoozing off or something. I don't seem to crave a nap now.

I feel engaged for the day. I feel excited for the day. I feel like I have all the energy for what I need to get done, working with my clients, and managing our business.

I feel like I've got all the focus and energy that I need to be successful. I'm not procrastinating on big key responsibilities anymore. And you know, when it comes to 4, 5, 6, 7 p.m., I don't feel like I just need to crash on the couch.

When it's time to spend time with my wife, I have the energy, and the focus, and the positive outlook to engage with her in conversation about our business, or her day, or what our plans are.

It's just a night and day change from where I was. I don't feel like when I get done with work that I just have to physically shut down. I don't have that anymore."

— Chris A., Texas, Business Owner

CASE STUDY
Andy M., North Carolina, High-Level Executive

"I feel like I have been reborn into the life I always intended to lead."

Introduction: Andy had a huge driving force behind his decision to get his health back in order: his two sons.

He dreamed of being an active and engaged father to his boys, but as most men experience, certain situations in life can get in the way of those dreams and goals.

He was focused on his job and spent his spare time trying to "catch up" to put more of his energy into his career. The professional pressure combined with his family responsibilities wore him out.

He felt guilty for being so run down and always felt torn between work and family.

He knew something had to change to regain this precious time with his children.

After Andy went through the program and stayed committed to the structure of the methods, here's what he said:

"I wanted to share something with the group. Prior to starting this journey just over six months ago, I wasn't nearly as engaged in the lives of my family as I am today.

Tough to admit it, but it's the truth.

Years ago, I envisioned myself being a very active dad/ family man but ultimately lacked the energy to truly be present for them.

There have been numerous benefits to getting my health in order, but none bigger to me than having the energy I have now... which has helped me be the father that I knew I could be.

Today, my two boys had a flag football game, and I coached their team. That's something I would have passed up before.

Six months ago, I would have likely been napping on the couch, missing these precious moments in life, thinking I needed to catch up on rest, so I could plow everything I had into my job.

Nowadays, not a chance... I wouldn't miss this for the world!

Very thankful to have placed a bet on Logan Henry many months ago.

I feel like I have been reborn into the life I always intended to lead."

— Andy M., North Carolina, High-Level Executive

**The last names of clients have been redacted to protect their privacy. For serious prospects wanting to work directly with me who would like more in-depth information and verification of results, please reach out to me or my team by going to https://www.acceleratedmethod.com/call*

Amazing, right?

Did you see yourself in these stories?

I hope you did. Because I want to help you write your own story, just like these guys.

It all starts within the pages of this book. I'm sharing *all* my secrets with you.

Why?

I found someone who let me in and shared his health secrets with me. His name was Greg. And his guidance and strategies changed my life.

Greg was my lifeline. It's my personal mission to help

you regain your edge, the way Greg helped me. And "paying it forward" doesn't get better than this!

Now, I get to enjoy my life. I bounce out of bed and work with guys just like you!

High-performers with a desire to be everything they can be to everyone they love. The ripple effect of what you do with the information in this book is massive and will continue into all areas of your life.

But it's not guaranteed.

Do you want to know the biggest reason some guys read a few pages from this book, but then never do anything about it?

It's not for lack of desire, I can tell you that!

Look, I get emails and messages every day from men just like you who find the information in this book really helpful and, dare I say, damn exciting.

I mean, who doesn't want to shed those embarrassing "love handles," sleep better, and recapture all the energy they had from their early 20s?

So I get it. Every guy who reads this book starts with good intentions.

But sometimes it feels like taking care of ourselves fully is one thing too many on our list of things to do.

When that happens, we either quit or we get help, not only to implement changes in how we think and live, but to hold our feet to the fire a little, and remind us why we're doing this.

That's where I come in. I work with guys like you every day. What I can tell you is everyone of them is different, starting from a different place with different needs. This is why step one is finding out about THEIR situation, (believe me, I've seen it all), and meeting them where they're at.

With that in mind, as you read this book, know I'm here to help you put all the pieces together, get your health sorted once and for all, and regain your edge.

Here's the link: *https://www.acceleratedmethod.com/call*

Together we'll map out your plan and make it happen.

Key Chapter Takeaways

I use two core principles to get your mind and body back to how they used to be:

Principle #1: Start Where You Are. If you're depleted, nothing you sign up for is going to work unless the first area of focus is bringing you out of the red and at least to neutral.

Principle #2: Sustainability. The key to long-term health and wellness is not to hate the process. The goal is to find a method that works for you and seamlessly fits into your lifestyle.

There are other men, just like you, who have been exactly where you are right now. They used the information in this book, and worked with me to implement a sustainable health practice and changed their lives for the better.

CHAPTER 2

Is This Right For You?

You ever look at a photo and think to yourself:

"No way that's me..."

Well, those are pretty much the exact words I said to myself over 12 years ago after seeing a picture a family member had taken of me while on vacation.

My fake, over-stretched smile said it all.

So did the gut hanging over my belt, (despite my best efforts to disguise it with dark shades of clothing).

I was exhausted on a daily basis, doing my best to get through work until I could make it home and crash on the couch.

"I'll start tomorrow," I kept telling myself.

You can imagine how effective that line of thinking was.

Despite my best efforts, I would go through my day in a mental fog, taking way longer to get things done than I should have.

I would constantly push important tasks back to the next day... and then the next day...

My personal standards were dropping, and my blood pressure was rising.

My physical confidence… Wait, *what* physical confidence?

I constantly covered up my insecurities with things like drinking, insincere laughter, or mindless eating, (including way too many fast food runs).

Anything to suppress how I was really feeling, which was ***miserable.***

I'd had ENOUGH.

I felt: Weak. Soft. Powerless.

It was really frustrating to have clothes not fit me the way they used to.

Or to have to think about grabbing a T-shirt every time I went to the beach because I no longer felt okay about the way my body looked — *especially* in front of other people, (including my beautiful wife).

And though I was good at putting up a front around others, cracking jokes, and acting like everything was just fine…

Truth was, I was embarrassed.

I knew something had to change…and fast.

But it wasn't until I was able to be honest with myself and take full responsibility before things finally shifted.

It's one of the many reasons I understand my clients so well.

They, too, have gotten to the point where they've had ENOUGH.

Can you relate? Maybe even just a little?

Guys come to me all the time because they're tired of feeling ...

... exhausted and not having the energy after a long work day to enjoy life with their family and loved ones.

... embarrassed about their outward appearance and feeling less desirable to their partners.

... winded every time they walk upstairs, tie their shoes, or play ball with their kids.

... anxious looking at the clothes in their closet, wondering how much longer they'll be able to fit into their favorite shirt before they have to order another size up.

... constantly stressed and taking that stress out on their wife, their kids, or their work colleagues, without meaning to.

... regret over all the opportunities they've missed out on both personally and professionally because they feel like they couldn't get their shit together when they should have.

Here's the thing...

As high performers, it's not in our nature to recognize when our bodies and minds are screaming at us to slow down and figure out why we feel lousy.

Instead, we constantly push ourselves to the next level, always driving hard to succeed. The natural thought is to: "Push through! Man up! Pull it together."

Look, I get it. I hated the idea of slowing down long enough to figure out how to get healthy. My life and work schedule were so busy, how could I find time to exercise, let alone figure out what to eat, how to prep it, etc?

It was at that point that I was lucky enough to find my own health mentor.

And it was in going through my own transformation that I became inspired by the strategies I had learned to help others do the same. It's been my singular professional passion ever since.

I committed to my own personal growth 100 percent, and finally found the solution that ended the start/stop cycles for good.

Here's what happened incrementally when I applied this solution to my life:

- I felt a renewed clarity and focus. My energy went up dramatically. And this all happened immediately, in the first days! This created a positive spiral effect on my motivation as my body and mind adapted to my "new" normal.
- I actually lost weight without starving myself OR

eating rabbit food. I was full, satisfied, and shedding pounds.

- The quality of my sleep improved dramatically. I stopped dragging myself out of bed in the morning. And "The 3 p.m. Slump" became a thing of the past.
- My mood improved! Irritability and "edginess" are common issues in overworked and depleted men, and I had been no different. However, because of the cascading effects of increased energy, weight loss, better meal habits, and improved sleep quality, I reacted in much healthier ways to the world around me. I was much more even keeled, and problems that previously would have frustrated me to no end now no longer bothered me. The old me was back!
- With my mind and body clear, my productivity skyrocketed! Planning became easier, I became more systematic, and I now hit my deadlines with ease.

Here's what I want you to understand: What I'm really teaching you in these pages is a sustainable lifestyle for an unbridled life of achievement and joy.

This is NOT a "get-fit-quick" scheme. And this is NOT designed to punish you for your previous health choices.

If you're willing to commit to real change, this method will be the last stop on your journey to the happy, healthy future that's always been waiting for you.

Do you want to know what the most powerful thing you can do RIGHT NOW to move your health forward is?

It's this: **Address your depleted energy levels by learning how to say no and slow down.**

Here's why this is so critical: Stress and burnout are common symptoms of *chasing your day* versus *controlling the outcomes* of your day.

Controlling the outcomes of your day means you don't let your schedule or your goals be the master over you. You don't have to start with rehashing your entire schedule. You can start small. Whatever you do, start today.

"Okay," I can hear you say, "That's all very well, but start *WHERE* exactly?"

Hang tight, we're getting there!

But first ... since this chapter is titled, "Is This Right for You?" I want to make sure we're on the same page and that you can give yourself a clear assessment of where you are right now.

Because you have to know where you're starting from if you want to reach your destination.

In the next chapter, I'll be equipping you with some simple and practical strategies to help you begin to resolve your depleted energy levels.

But let's quickly review your current situation. Read the following statements and see how many of them ring true for you:

- You probably wake up most mornings feeling groggy and out of sorts. Hitting a wall of tiredness in the afternoon, feeling like you have to take a nap just to get through the rest of the day, (but instead you grab that 2 pm cup of coffee).

- It's hard to be "switched on" all the time to be the best possible boss and leader at work, then collapsing into the couch as soon as you get home with little left in the tank to engage and be present with your loved ones.
- You most likely experience brain fog and lack the stamina and mental sharpness to produce at your highest level.
- You try to put on a good front and fake it as best as you can, pretending everything is ok, while you secretly suspect the people around you are starting to wonder what's going on with you.
- You feel like your self-confidence has plummeted and that you've lost your edge.
- You avoid long pauses in front of the mirror because you're not proud of the guy staring back at you.
- You probably feel like you don't have the fire in your belly to truly move the needle on your biggest hopes and dreams.
- You really hate choosing what clothes to wear based on hiding problem areas rather than wearing what you like. Feeling frustrated that none of your favorite clothes fit like they used to.
- You feel like you're doing the right thing when

you spend thousands on nice beach vacations to destress from work, yet you dread it at the same time because the idea of taking your shirt off in public equals embarrassment.

- You know you're being impatient, short, and grumpy with the most important people in your life.
- You also know you're missing out on memorable experiences, (not to mention various opportunities), because you feel drained all the time.
- You feel annoyed with yourself when you get out of breath after climbing a flight of stairs.
- Mainly, you're worried about the health risks that may be lurking around the corner.

And most frustrating of all: you've been working hard for the last 10 to 20 years to become successful in the outside world, but on the inside, you've realized you sacrificed yourself to get there.

Now, does ANY of the above sound familiar to you? If so, even if it's a few of them, then know that you're in the right place reading this book.

Believe me, I've been there…

One day you look in the mirror and don't quite recognize the guy staring back at you.

Energy, health, confidence, clarity, and focus…

Gone.

It's not an ideal situation. And I wouldn't wish that on anyone.

I've helped hundreds of successful high achievers for the past ten years, and this is what I see over and over...

Hard-driving, well-meaning guys burning the candle at both ends literally sick and tired of being sick and tired.

What makes things even worse?

The routines and methods that might have worked back in your 20's simply don't work like they used to, (if at all). Not to mention, most so-called solutions out there are either aimed to beat you down, starve you to death, or take over your entire life. Which stacks even more of a problem onto your already overloaded plate.

Perhaps you've tried some of the following: Personal Trainers, Fad Diets, at Home Workout DVDs or Cycling Bikes, Brutalizing and Boring Workout Programs, Hardcore Bootcamps, Unsustainable Quick Fixes, B-12 Shots, Supplements, Keto, Low Carb, the latest Hype Cardio Gym up the road.

Or maybe you've been told to get into Beast Mode or become some kind of cross fitter, (which doesn't appeal nor do you have the time or capacity to do it).

Here's the thing, I'm not saying all that stuff is bad. For some men, it works. And that's great.

But from my experience, it's not always what works and what doesn't. *It's about what fits a person's lifestyle the best.*

The fact is, this is probably not your fault.

Being a successful businessman and high-performer can be hard.

In between keeping employees, clients, partners, and team members happy, then managing payroll, taxes, ensuring profits are going up, (and pile on trying to balance all the other balls you have up in the air)...

It's perfectly understandable how you may have unintentionally put yourself and your health on the back burner.

You might be wondering, "How do I find the time to take care of myself with the little time and energy that I do have?"

That's the beauty of The Accelerated Method.

Our mission here is to build a personal strategy that works specifically for you, that helps you get back the body, energy, stamina, and strength you had in your younger years. *We're going to do that in a way that doesn't interfere or overload everything else you already have on your plate.*

My primary goal in writing this book is to help you get your life and body back. To introduce a sustainable way of living that isn't riddled with resistance, gym memberships, and the latest diets. You don't need those things. Instead, you need a simple plan, easily executed and repeated, that's built on the deep principles of men's health.

Before we continue, let me be clear about something important ...

I'm not just some run-of-the-mill coach who only cares about physical fitness.

You can think of me as more of a "time travel" service for men.

As in: I help men turn back the clock, reversing time so that they can return back to their stronger, youthful selves, (without any of the youthful mistakes we all made back then)!

What I do — and what you'll find on the pages of this book — goes well beyond the physical.

It's designed to address *your entire being*, and we do it with a holistic approach that's as practical as it is effective.

Imagine waking up each day with boundless energy, a physical presence that turns heads, confidence that commands attention, a laser-like focus that allows you to accomplish more in less time, and a calm demeanor that makes you a pleasure to be around even in the midst of chaos.

These are the results my clients have come to expect. And it's all thanks to the specialized system and tailored approach I take with each and every guy who chooses to work with me.

So what can you expect if you not only read, but *apply*, what's in these pages?

Well, rather than promising over-hyped results, let me give it to you straight: By applying what you're about to see, you can expect to feel *at least* 50 percent better — if not more — *immediately*.

Now, 50 percent might not sound like a lot. But remember, it's an *immediate* improvement and quite significant. Why? Because that's enough to move the needle. And it will be enough to motivate you to continue. Which is crucial because by taking consistent and frequent action, that 50 percent will eventually lead to 100 percent over time. (I have guys who report that they feel 200 or 300 percent better; it all depends on where you're starting from and whether you're willing to put in the effort.)

That's right- I won't sugarcoat it. This journey requires commitment, effort, and a willingness to step out of one's comfort zone.

It's not for everyone, and that's okay. But if you're ready to elevate your entire life and not settle for "what is" but strive for "what could be," then I invite you to read on to discover the potential for change that lies within you.

Key Chapter Takeaways

- What I'm really teaching you in these pages is a sustainable lifestyle for an unbridled life of achievement and joy.
- Address your depleted energy levels by learning how to say no and slow down. (I'll be showing you how in the next chapter.)

- It's not about what exercise/nutrition/health approaches work, it's about what fits into your lifestyle.

CASE STUDY

Dusty G, South Carolina, High-Level Executive and Business Owner

From out of shape and exhausted to accomplished and energized

"Before, I was busy, not taking time for myself, and I let myself go. I was out of shape, feeling tired. I was 43 years old but I felt like I was 60. I felt like I was maybe neglecting my wife and kids. I wanted to get in shape so that I could work a long day, come home, and still have enough energy to spend time with them and do fun things on the weekends. At that point, I was ten years into my business, and I put every bit of effort into creating my business.

By the time I met Logan, I was searching for some kind of way forward. He's definitely changed my life. And you know, I've met a lot of people and come across lots of different programs. But looking back into all my adult years, he's the one guy that was able to show me the difference and show me the results. That's what I was looking for.

Before starting I was 242 pounds and today I'm 195 pounds. There were gains I ended up seeing that I never counted on. I didn't realize what it would do for my mind.

I kind of figured it would help my relationships with my wife and kids but that's even gone above and beyond what I expected. I now have more time in my day, and that's because I don't spend 10 or 12 hours at work and then 3 or 4 more hours sitting in the chair watching TV eating potato chips, just too exhausted to move, and then go to bed and then start the whole cycle over the next day. The amount of things I accomplish in my work day now are far beyond what I used to be capable of. I leave work at the end of the day, I'm not exhausted, and I feel like- let's go do something else, let's start another activity. I sleep six to seven hours a night, and I wake up feeling great. I've learned that I don't have time not to do what I'm doing.

To sum it up, I can't believe what I've gotten done since I started the program. And it's not just from a business standpoint. It's my family. It's my physical well-being. It's my mental well-being. It definitely has been life changing."

— Dusty G., South Carolina, High-Level Executive and Business Owner

CHAPTER 3

The Six Common Roadblocks to 'Getting The Old You Back' and How to Overcome Them

Over the last decade, I've helped my clients lose more than 2,156 pounds collectively. The men I have worked with have improved their sleep habits, energy levels, personal relationships, work performance, and overall health.

The reason my methods work is because I meet you where you are at, plain and simple, (more on that in the next chapter).

I've seen men try and fail, and try again. I've seen what works. I know what doesn't.

Which is why I'd like to share with you six roadblocks that my clients have stumbled on in their health journey. Rest assured, my framework addresses each of these roadblocks specifically. The remedies are baked right into the fabric of everything I teach.

Since you're reading this book, I'm going to assume you'll recognize most, if not all, of these roadblocks. Let me take it a step further than identification. Let's take a look at each one and see where you rate. Then I'll show you how to solve them.

Let's get you back to being you!

ROADBLOCK #1: Not Enough Time

Some days, it seems as if all we're doing is racing against the clock from the moment we wake up.

As soon as your feet hit the floor, you are living and breathing by the calendar app on your phone. Constant notifications, emails, and calls bombard you. A fire here… an opinion there… the promise of a "quick" call that turns into a lost hour and several items added to your to-do list.

Emails, texts, meetings, Zoom calls, conference calls, clients, customers, coworkers, family, events, errands, appointments. The list goes on.

Are you feeling tense? 'Cause I am just writing this!

It's no wonder your go-to answer when asked about your health goals is, "I'll do it when I have some extra time." Or, "I'll start working out when this project wraps up / my kids go to camp / holidays are over / family stuff settles down / little league coaching is over/ etc…"

"When I have time" is the biggest lie we tell ourselves.

It's not just that your to-do list is long. It's that the expectations you set for yourself are intense. The lure of waiting for the "right time" is a trap that's kept you treading water, head barely above the surface.

It's easy to feel hopeless in such circumstances.

The goal here is to rework your day in 2 simple ways.

1. Start by recognizing the difference between productive time vs. lost time in the course of your day. To do that, answer these questions:

   - How long do you spend rewriting emails or proposals because you can't get your thoughts together?
   - Are you running back to the grocery store because you forgot something on your list?
   - What are you trading when you "catch up on sleep" by napping in the evenings and weekends?

2. Create a structured morning routine that sets you up for success. This will determine what your day will look and feel like. This gives you time to "put on your oxygen mask," which is an important concept we'll discuss in Chapter 6.

The critical issue here is simple: Are you controlling your day, or is your day controlling you?

☑ Success Check-in Exercise

Before we proceed with the rest of the book, let's first check in with where you're at right now with the intensity of your day-to-day schedule.

Below, rate yourself on a scale from 1-5 on how accurate

the statements are. 1 means "not accurate at all," and 5 means "most accurate."

Once you've rated yourself for each statement, total up your scores and then use the Answer Key to determine your next steps.

Statement	Your Score
I'm often sleeping through my alarm clock and starting my day in a rush.	
I pick up my phone the moment I get out of bed to see what's in my inbox or messages and check my daily calendar.	
Time seems to move very quickly during the day, and I'm constantly trying to chase time.	
The only quiet time I have is in the car or the bathroom.	
I always feel like I need to be in two places at once.	
I feel guilty saying no to work or personal requests.	
I often find that my mental clarity gets foggier throughout the day. By 3 p.m. I can't think straight.	

I barely have time to eat lunch.	
I am working later because I can't get everything done during the day.	
I wish I had a "pause" button for life so I could just take a freakin' break!	
TOTAL UP YOUR SCORE	

What Your Score Really Means

Score: 10 - 15
Busy But Manageable

Your days are busy, but you know what needs to get done, and you do it.

There are times when you are handling a lot, but you know that giving your all for a short period of time will keep everything on track.

Take a look at the first steps outlined after this section and rely on these as your fundamentals in maintaining a grip on your time.

Just be mindful of how quickly you can go from "I've got this" to "How am I going to get all of this done?"

Score: 16 - 35
Racing Through Your Day

If you are in this zone, then you are reaching a breaking point. Your days are intense, and you are juggling way too many things.

You are managing it all right now, but things may start to slip at work and home very soon. You may be noticing that your family is being affected by your busy schedule as well. You are working late nights and feeling way more run down than you ever have been.

There is constant pressure to keep going and maintain your edge, but you are feeling the effects of stress on your mental and physical state.

First, implement the "first steps" as outlined at the end of this section. Second, continue reading and pay particular attention to Chapter 4 where I address what I call "Health Debt" and what that means for your personal and professional life.

Score: 36+
You've Exceeded Max Capacity

It's time to take a hard look at what's going on in work and life. The blunt truth is that your days are controlling you, not the other way around.

You need to find ways to create some space in your calendar, in your workday, and more time for you and your family.

As hard as it may feel at first, implement the first steps at the end of this section. It's time to start delegating tasks to reliable coworkers. To create some positive change in the work environment so you don't feel like it's all on you.

What things can you stop doing and/or say no to? You don't have to handle everything on your own.

If you continue this way, you will completely burn out.

Take heart, the strategies in this book will bring you back into equilibrium with the demands on your time.

What to Start with Right Now:

Begin taking control of your day by doing the following:

- Categorize the tasks in your day by "productive time" and "lost time". Keep a record of it. Delegate and adjust as needed.
- Get up when your alarm goes off. No more snooze button!
- Spend 10-15 seconds (at least) in cold water during your morning shower. Cold exposure increases focus and energy as you warm up from the cold. Start by taking your warm shower and then for the last 10 to 20 seconds, turn the water to cold. Once you've done that for a few days, I challenge you to add just 10 more seconds each day until you're able to finish up to 30 to 60 seconds. This will increase circulation and jumpstart your body and mind. Seriously, give this a try even if you don't want to. You will feel AMAZING when you step out of the shower!

ROADBLOCK #2: Not Enough Energy

How many times have you rolled up your sleeves, grabbed another cup of coffee, and "pushed through" a project or family responsibility in the last month alone?

I can hear you saying, "Now why would that be a bad thing?"

Why, indeed?

Well, truth be told, it's not *completely* a bad thing. I'm not advocating for a life of leisure and stagnation. Look, I'm just like you ... you're talking to a fellow high performer here. I'm continually moving, pushing, persevering, reaching – that's in our DNA.

However ...

What I won't accept is pushing yourself so hard that you burn out and collapse.

The "Don't stop when you're tired, stop when you're done!" mentality is born from the hustle and grind crowd. A crowd that doesn't care where you're at in six months, and that doesn't take into account the dream retirement you're working toward in the next decade. "Hustle and grind" is all about the here and now with no sight for future consequences.

That's a recipe for disaster.

Here's what that looks like: high blood pressure, digestive issues, ED, insomnia, stress, fatigue, diabetes, and so much more. The constant pressures are endless. And the hustle and grind approach only makes these issues worse.

If you're already feeling depleted, running on fumes, your bones and soul completely exhausted, then my very first goal for you is to get your energy back.

Here's the truth: I can help you become the best version of yourself, but if you are starting from a place of depletion, it simply won't work.

You must make adjustments, or you'll never get your life back.

You need to move past hustle and grind. Now is the time to work smarter and set up a holistically enjoyable existence.

✔ Success Check-in Exercise

Before we proceed with the rest of the book, let's first check in with where you're at right now with your energy levels.

Below, rate yourself on a scale from 1-5 on how accurate the statements are. 1 means "not accurate at all," and 5 means "most accurate."

Once you've rated yourself for each statement, total up your scores and then use the Answer Key to determine your next steps.

Success Check-In Statement	Self-Rating
It's really difficult to get up in the morning and get myself going.	
I don't start to "wake up" until I've had at least two cups of coffee.	
My mornings are productive, but by lunchtime, I start to fade and get tired.	
I drag in the afternoons into the evening.	
By the time I get home from work, I have nothing left and look forward to doing nothing.	
If there are evening family activities (i.e., driving to sports practice, events, gatherings), I have to force myself to get up and go.	
I can easily doze off when I'm at home and nap often on weekends.	
I used to look forward to doing fun activities and going on adventures, but now I just want to do nothing.	

I worry that I'm missing out on so much in my life, but I can't find the motivation to change anything.	
I miss that boundless energy I used to have when I was younger.	
TOTAL UP YOUR SCORE	

What Your Score Really Means

Score: 10 - 15
Even though you have a lot going on in your life, you still have enough energy to get stuff done. You are working and spending time with your family. You may even be finding time for personal interests and trying new things.

Treat the "first steps" at the end of this section as your fundamentals to maintaining your energy levels.

Score: 16 - 35
Your energy is really low most days. Depending on what your day is like, you may find that you'll have long bursts of energy and productivity, but they may be short-lived.

You're starting to realize at what points of the day you will be at your best and when you're at your worst.

You notice that you want more downtime and rest and that your stamina isn't like it used to be.

Maybe you're not as interested in outside activities

and look forward to puttering around the house on the weekends.

Implement the "first steps" at the end of this section. What you may find is that you're not missing anything from these fundamentals, but you haven't been educated on the effects of your body's natural hormone composition and the role of inflammation. We address both of these topics in Chapter 5.

Score: 36+

If you are in this section, you are ready for a complete life-style change. You are now really sick of feeling lousy. Your outlook may feel bleak, and you may be frustrated and moody.

You know this isn't you. You don't even recognize yourself. It's as if you are living in someone else's body.

Okay, so how do we fix this? That's what we're here for, after all!

Let me sketch out in broad strokes what to start implementing, and then I'll give you a single specific action step you can start doing right now.

Here are the things you should start addressing immediately so that you can get back to feeling like you again:

1. Do whatever you have to do to start getting some really good sleep.

2. Schedule a day (or two) off and block that time out. No phone. No laptop. No "checking-in." No family activities. Just spend the day and regroup.
3. Rearrange your calendar and get rid of anything you don't want to do or don't need to do. If you dread doing something, step away from it. I personally live by the "Hell Yes" method, and I recommend you do, too. It works like this: If you're trying to decide whether to do something, ask yourself if it's a "HELL YES" or not. If it's not, then ditch it. Simple, right? But it works! It also ensures that you live life on YOUR happiest terms.
4. Allow yourself "you" time. Mornings are best.
5. Nourish your body with good foods.
6. Have fun!

What to Start with Right Now:

If a lack of energy has you drowning in your day-to-day, here's something you can start doing *today*:

- Make a list of everything that requires your attention regularly. Decide what you want to continue and what you want to let go. Step back from any obligations that don't move you closer to the Ideal You. Be ruthless! If you're going to take back control of your life, be decisive and prioritize what will work for YOU.

- For those things that aren't serving you, delegate. Hire someone to mow the lawn if you hate it. Step down from the board that is draining you. Cut. Delegate. Let go.

Just doing this one thing will make a huge difference, trust me. Heck, even just making the list will make you feel better! (But don't stop there, follow through on it!) Feeling depleted is serious business, and if you don't address it now, you could be headed for trouble. The above will resolve it, but it does require follow-through.

Roadblock #3: Unsustainable Expectations

Here are the expectations on your shoulders as a high performer in your stage of life: Be The Provider, The Protector, The Rescuer, and The Rock everyone leans on... AND not only that, but make sure you're successful in all these things!

That's a tall order. And it comes with a heavy price...

The more you give to that goal, the more you sacrifice, the more you accomplish, the more you soldier on in the midst of physical and mental pain... the more of a man you are, right?

And I know you, you don't complain about it. You hustle, you sacrifice. You put in more hours at work than at home to make sure there is a home for your family.

And at the same time, you try to make time for what is most important: your family. You attend recitals. Mow the lawn. Catch a cat nap while "watching" a cartoon with your son or daughter so you can get up and do it all over again.

When the thought crosses your mind to ask for a break, to request time at the gym, to simply ask for a little bit of help and grace... you dismiss it as selfish.

It's easy to think that it's selfish to spend time on something that has no bearing on your role as provider, protector, rescuer, or rock. So you continue on in the same way you have been, convinced you just need to "man up" a little more.

This, by the way, is why you feel sick and tired of being sick and tired. And it is unquestionably the road that leads to divorce, inescapable stress, and a likely earlier-than-necessary death.

You're holding expectations for your role at work and your role at home, two places that you are fully committed to, and rightly so. You provide for your family and bringing home the bacon allows you to protect your family's stability. At home you're the spider-killer, the rescuer, and the rock when your teenager needs wisdom and a hug.

You can't let go of either of these things.

But what if I told you that you don't have to?

Dig a little deeper and find the common denominator here... YOU.

You are the one who is present at work. You are the one

with these roles in your home. And whether or not you realize it, you are making choices every single day that keep you stuck in this never-ending cycle of depletion.

This is where the notion of “counter culture” comes in, so named because it flies in the face of the current societal narratives that keep you chained to this unsustainable loop.

You want to be a real man? One that shows up in all the areas of your life? Great. I’ll help you get there without needing a catnap on the weekends.

You want to give more freely of your time and energy without feeling resentment or only showing up out of obligation? Fantastic. Then keep reading and make the changes you know you want to make.

If you feel constricted by the expectations in your life, I promise this one simple step is the beginning of a different, better, you: Schedule 30 minutes for yourself every morning. Put it in your calendar. No meetings. No work emails. No “doomscrolling” social media or various websites to catch up on bad news.

This will be hard to do at first. Habit can be a tough enemy! But if you stick with it, I promise you’ll experience the profound benefit in store for you.

Breathe and exist. Prioritize yourself first thing in the morning, and you will have more of yourself to give to those roles in your life you cherish, (more on this in Chapter 6).

The truth is found in the simple things because:

1) Simplicity moves the needle far more than any complicated battle plan, and 2) The simple things are the most important because they are the most easily overlooked.

Self-care, the focus on your own physical and mental well-being, is an undiluted, powerful principle that lies at the heart of any healthy high performer.

Take control of your day, delegate the tasks that don't support the ideal version of you, and schedule a damn 30-minute window for yourself.

☑ Success Check-in Exercise

Before we proceed with the rest of the book, let's first check in with where you're at right now in terms of your energy and motivation levels.

Below, rate yourself on a scale from 1-5 on how accurate the statements are. 1 means "not accurate at all," and 5 means "most accurate."

Once you've rated yourself for each statement, total up your scores and then use the Answer Key to determine your next steps.

Success Check-In Statement	Self-Rating
I need to drink coffee throughout the day to keep myself going.	
I feel tired to my core.	
Even if I get a good night's sleep, I still wake up feeling tired.	
I don't have the same enthusiasm for work and life as I did before.	
Everything feels like it's on my shoulders.	
I hardly ever laugh.	
I often think, "If I don't do it, no one will."	
Sometimes I think about taking a midday nap in my car.	
I feel guilty because my kids want to play when I get home, but I don't have the energy.	
I used to have the drive to get big projects started at work, but now it feels like a huge undertaking.	
TOTAL UP YOUR SCORE	

What Your Score Really Means

Score: 10 - 15

You may have days where you feel more run down than others, but overall, your energy levels are fairly consistent.

Some days you may feel like there are too many to-dos or tasks to get done, but if you stay later at work here and there, you can get it under control.

You have a healthy balance between what you expect of yourself and managing the expectations of others at work and home.

Treat the "first step" at the end of this section as your fundamental. Time to yourself will maintain the healthy balance you have struck.

Score: 16 - 35

Your days are consistently busy and full. Your calendar has very little give to it, and you are also navigating family responsibilities.

There is a pull between work and family, but somehow you are making it work. You may be missing a meeting or an event now and then, but you can find ways to make that up.

You feel wiped out by the end of the day, but you still feel as though you were mostly productive and on point.

If you are in this section, you are managing work and

family well, but there is zero time left over for yourself or other fun activities. Those get pushed off.

You will benefit from starting with the "first step" at the end of this section. Combined with other strategies in this book, you will improve the overall balance of your life.

Score: 36+

You are in desperate need of a schedule/life/calendar makeover. Right now, there are too many things pulling at you and demanding your attention.

This is a dangerous situation to be in because you are dancing around the edges of burnout.

It's time for a major overhaul in how much you say "yes" to during the day and all of these things you are involved in that you don't need to be.

One of the main reasons your energy levels are so low is because you are running on empty, without stopping to refuel. (Yes, I'm going to throw out a car analogy.) What happens when your car runs out of gas? You're stuck, and you're not moving. It's the same with you.

Schedule two days on your calendar to clean off your plate and restart. Start by implementing the strategies outlined in the time and energy roadblocks. Then add in the first step recommended at the end of this section.

What to Start with Right Now:

- Schedule a 30-minute window for yourself every day. No matter what. Put it in your calendar now, and call it "Meetup." As far as the world is concerned, you're in a meeting. With you. Do not disturb.

Roadblock #4: The Struggle to Make Healthy Food Choices

Many men I work with come with the expectation that they'll need to cut any enjoyable food out of their life. They believe it's time to starve themselves if they're really committed to their health journey.

And I can't blame them. The messages we get from many so-called "experts" in the health industry sing the praises of starvation diets and the rabbit-food-only diets.

If you've struggled with food, this mentality is a key reason you haven't seen much success in the past.

Any fitness or nutrition program that asks you to cut out meals or eat much less than your body needs means you are set up to fail before you have begun. Period. Full stop.

Liquid-only diets, fasting, and the like can work for some, (if done correctly). The key is to do it in a way that doesn't completely deprive the body of what it needs to thrive.

But before you start counting calories and slashing all your dinners from your family's meal plan, you first need to understand your relationship with food.

So let me ask you a couple of questions:

Does food comfort you after a hard day? You wouldn't be the only one! Look, we ALL have foods that make us feel better. Is it a bag of Doritos as you head for the couch for some ESPN? Or perhaps a sugar bomb quart of Ben & Jerry's right before bed?

Whatever it is, you probably have convinced yourself that in order to "feel better," you need (and deserve) that food. Which makes it challenging ***not*** to have those foods when you need some comfort.

The good news is, there's some science behind this behavior.

I'll spare you the explanations about dopamine receptors and metabolic pathways and just give you the short version as it might appear in a "breaking news" headline:

Comfort Foods Make Us Feel Better — Because of Some Very Compelling Biological and Emotional Reasons.

So remember this: When you decide to make dietary changes, **you will need to give yourself some forgiveness if it feels tough to let go of your comfort foods.**

It's not that you are failing or not "strong" enough to overcome those cravings. You barely stood a chance in the first place! That's because your brain and chemical processes are screaming at you to "comfort" them until you can find alternative "feel good" ways to regulate your systems.

In other words, give yourself a break. (But, don't think that means you have a license to keep doing it forever, either.) I'm here to teach you those alternatives so that you'll stop feeling the urge to go to the nutritional dark side on a regular basis.

Also, remember, there will be days that you may think, "Ah, screw it. I'll just eat [X] today and start again tomorrow." That's okay ... ***once in a while***. The point is to start again the next day in earnest and without beating yourself up over the relapse.

Breaking patterns with food is one of the most challenging areas in getting healthy. And look, this goes beyond chemical reactions in your brain and the inherent need for food. It could also be something triggered by a memory or an emotion, such as cake on a birthday or ice cream sundaes and barbecues in the summer. Or maybe it's pie simply because it reminds you of your grandmother.

Regardless, just recognizing these emotional triggers is an important first step. Be aware of those foods, their accompanying triggers, and then take an internal look at them by asking yourself: What other way could I connect to that memory *without* unhealthy food?

But of course: Enjoy that comfort food every now and then.

There's no reason to spend your entire life in deprivation and obsessive avoidance. That's no way to live, and it certainly will make you resentful of getting healthy and staying healthy. **The key to long-term health is to do the right things the vast majority of the time.**

Before we get to the Success Check-in for this section, ask yourself the following questions to help assess where you are on the issue of food as it relates to your health:

- Do you get "hangry" if you skip a meal?
- Does food bring you comfort after a challenging day? What foods specifically do you reach for when you want comfort?
- Does food equate to family and community for you?
- Is it a chore to eat? If you could take a magic pill to fuel you, would you take it, or do you actually enjoy eating?
- Do you love or hate to cook?

Understanding your relationship with food helps you set up and sustain a fitness and nutrition plan more efficiently.

Food can either fuel or drain you.

And as a side note, the concept of comfort food is rooted firmly in science.

I'll spare you the actual scientific data, but just know this: It's not all in your head — comfort food really does make us feel better.

This is one of the most common traps that causes guys to "fall off the wagon" after a hard day.

Simply having this awareness is the first step in solving it.

And again, I'm here to tell you: It's not entirely your fault. It's human. It's rooted in the elements that make up your very being. So be a little easier on yourself and start with the following assessment to start shedding light on your relationship with food.

✔ Success Check-in Exercise

Before we proceed with the rest of the book, let's first check in with where you're at right now in terms of your relationship with food.

Below, rate yourself on a scale from 1-5 on how accurate the statements are. 1 means "not accurate at all," and 5 means "most accurate."

Once you've rated yourself for each statement, total up your scores and then use the Answer Key to determine your next steps.

Success Check-In Statement	Self-Rating
I need something sweet or salty at the end of the day.	
I crave pasta or bread when I'm feeling stressed.	

I tell myself I'm only going to have a little bit of ice cream but end up eating most of the pint before bed.	
I have no willpower if there are snacks or sweets in our house.	
After a long, stressful day, I just want to crash in front of the TV with food.	
I grew up with the "clean your plate" messaging.	
When I'm feeling run down or my mood is low, I don't want something "healthy."	
It's hard for me to do portion control.	
I would consider myself a foodie.	
I don't have the energy to cook or figure out what to eat, so I get fast food.	
TOTAL UP YOUR SCORE	

What Your Score Really Means

Score: 10 - 15

You have a good relationship with food and snacks. You may treat yourself now and then, but you also know that there is a balance with food.

You probably follow the 80/20 rule of eating. 80 percent of the week, you are mindful of healthy eating, and 20 percent is the splurge.

If you are in your forties or are approaching your forties, you'll want to pay particular attention to Chapter 5 where I address changing hormones. Even those with very healthy habits can notice a dip in energy levels, experience disrupted sleep, and other mental and physical changes.

Score: 16 - 35

Food can be a challenge for you with regards to wanting to "feel better." You may reach for those snacks or ice cream during the day or in the evening in front of the TV.

Snacking is an issue because you are so busy that sometimes you don't have enough time to make or get something to eat, so you rely on quick-fix meals.

Those quick fixes can be loaded with bad fats, high sodium, and a ton of sugar. You are probably snacking your way to poor health.

I cover more actions to take with food specifically in Chapter 8. For now, strive to simply be more aware of your relationship with food and the role food plays in your day-to-day.

Score: 36+

If you are in this zone, you need a plan for better nutrition. You may not realize how much your food intake is affecting your overall mental and physical well-being.

Junk food and processed foods impact your energy levels, waistline, mental clarity, sleep, and physiology.

One of the first places to start on your journey to better health is to remove as much "comfort" and junk food as possible.

Chapter 8 addresses nutrition more deeply, and I encourage you to pay particular attention to that chapter and the action points outlined there.

What to Start with Right Now:

- Take a good, hard look into your refrigerator, food cabinets, and pantry. Now, identify the foods you either don't love, or the ones you know aren't any good for you. You could even go ahead and tag them with a small piece of tape, take a snapshot of them with your phone, or mark them with a Sharpie — just do whatever's easiest for you to label them clearly in your own mind in the here and now for the sake of your own awareness. We'll be taking more actionable steps on this one later in the book. At this stage, the point is to just be keenly aware of them.

Why is awareness important at this stage?

Well, I've learned from experience that we can't fix what we don't even see in the first place.

And trust me, it's not your fault. We ALL do things throughout the day that we don't realize are bad. We're all running on autopilot to some extent.

And that's why with your nutrition, simply getting awareness is the all-important first step.

You can only change what you're willing to acknowledge first. Awareness precedes improvement 100 percent of the time. So take a good look in your fridge and cupboards and start getting CLARITY.

Roadblock #5: Overcoming Past Injuries & Bad Experiences

This isn't your first rodeo. I'm sure you've been here before. You've tried the cleanses, the diets, and the workout programs.

Many of my clients are (understandably) concerned about getting injured when they restart some sort of exercise plan. Or, if they're not thinking about getting injured, they're worried they might re-experience the incredible soreness and pain from brutal-style workout programs they may have tried in the past. It's a valid concern. After all, no one wants to walk around like the Tin Man for days after a workout, which means you can't blame anyone for hesitating to restart some sort of regimen if they think that's normal and necessary.

The good news is, "no pain no gain" is a big fallacy. It's NOT necessary. And it doesn't have to be that way. Not by a longshot. I'll get into that shortly.

In fact, not only can you still get incredible results *without* ever going into beast mode, but you can achieve "back on fire" status starting from pretty serious disadvantages.

Let me tell you about one of the men in my private Accelerated Method *(https://www.acceleratedmethod.com/ov)* program. Wayne earned himself the nickname, "The Step King," because he had an existing hernia doctors refused to operate on until he first lost some weight.

I know that doesn't explain the nickname, so let me tell you what happened.

When Wayne first entered the program, he wasn't able to do any of the specified movements I typically use for weight loss. So we worked together to figure out what kind of movement he was confident doing and, most importantly, what he would enjoy and consistently do.

He was open to the idea of walking. And so we nicknamed Wayne, "The Step King."

He dropped 31 pounds, his A1C dropped down half a point, and he dropped two full pant sizes. He's also sleeping better, waking up feeling like a million bucks, his energy has rebounded, and he doesn't feel the need to take naps anymore. Wayne can go all day.

Not surprisingly, his attitude has improved and his family, friends, and workers have all noticed the change in him.

But let's back up a second. I think it's important to look at exactly WHY guys get injured in the first place.

Most of my high-performing clients approach their fitness the same way they approach their work and life, ALL IN. I appreciate the "Let's do this!" mentality, but to go from little physical activity to intense workouts will cause your body to react poorly.

You'll wind up injured and in worse shape than you currently are because your body is not the same as it once was. It's a hard truth to swallow and one I need you to face head on.

Age, hormones, flexibility, and muscle strength all play a part in our ability to work out and recover. Willpower alone will not transform your body.

In fact, the most significant factor in injuries and pain from exercise is inflammation- a phenomenon I'll discuss more in depth in Chapter 5.

For now, please understand that you must work with your body in order to achieve the results you seek. This is a key part of my framework I've used to get hundreds of clients outstanding results in their health and wellness.

I often hear questions like this…

"Is this actually different from the other things I've tried? Isn't all health and wellness basically the same?"

"I've already sunk a ton of money into protein powders, supplements, muscle builders, etc. Are you going to make me buy more?"

Look, these are reasonable questions, but let's get clear about something right here:

I'm not a 20-something Instagram model with washboard abs who knows nothing about what REALLY matters to men over 40, and when you get right down to it, I'm talking about hormones, inflammation, and all the other hidden roadblocks that men face.

Unlike them, I can truly relate.

Because what I bring to the table is a decade of experience working shoulder to shoulder with high-performing men (like you) in their 40's and beyond. See, I'm no stranger to the unique challenges you face and I know the tailored solutions you need.

So forget those picture-perfect, 20-something fitness influencers with minimal responsibilities and heaps of time on their hands- insisting that "beast mode" is the answer to get your health in order.

Because here's the thing... they just don't get the pressures you face daily, nor can they relate to being pulled in a thousand different directions as you juggle life's many demands.

That's why what I offer instead is a genuine, customizable approach designed exclusively for ambitious guys like you, who know that age is just a number. I've spent years cracking the code so you can reignite that youthful fire and reawaken the physical prime that made you stand tall, strut with purpose, and tackle challenges with the swagger of a rockstar. And together, we'll dive into the nitty-gritty details of often-overlooked factors like hormones, inflammation, and the hidden obstacles that stand in your way.

I'm not here to get you a "beach body" for the summer. I'm not going to hand you a crash diet to get you ready for that wedding in three weeks.

This is not a short-term project for me.

I'm interested in your *long-term health*.

Now, don't get me wrong — I can certainly turn you into "The Fit Dad" at your daughter's wedding, or transform you into the silver fox of your next beach-front high school reunion, but please know, those are only nice byproducts in service to more important lifetime health goals.

I'm here to give you results that last longer than a spray tan.

I'm here to give you what truly matters.

I am here to get you sustainable, life-altering results. The kind of results that add years to your life and untold quality moments in the areas that matter.

As for supplements...

Any supplement I recommend is just that: a supplement. Not something to support a billion-dollar industry with the best direct response copywriters in the world.

Unsexy as it may seem, the key components to achieving your health goals are: eating the right foods, physical activity to keep your body functioning correctly, and restful, restorative sleep.

Supplements can then round out the edges.

No supplement will "fix" your health. None of the promised shortcuts of famous supplements are true.

What does work is creating a sustainable, easily-repeatable lifestyle that starts exactly where you are and steps you into the life you want. No beast-mode workouts. No crazy gym stunts that could make some orthopedic surgeon rich. No magic pills.

If past experiences are currently holding you back from getting started on your health and wellness goals, then I encourage you to take a few minutes to complete this assessment for specific recommendations on where to begin.

☑ Success Check-in Exercise

Before we proceed with the rest of the book, let's first check in with where you're at right now, physically.

Below, rate yourself on a scale from 1-5 on how accurate the statements are. 1 means "not accurate at all," and 5 means "most accurate."

Once you've rated yourself for each statement, total up your scores and then use the Answer Key to determine your next steps.

Success Check-In Statement	Self-Rating
I used to be very physically active, but now I don't have the time.	

My joints ache when I do too much physical activity.	
I have access to gym/exercise equipment and I don't use it.	
If I'm choosing between work and exercise, I always choose work.	
The last time I started working out again, I was in pain for days.	
I don't feel like I am as strong as I used to be.	
Working out at home is hard and so it's easy to put off doing.	
If there were an easy way to work out, I would do it.	
I don't even know what physical activity would help me lose weight.	
TOTAL UP YOUR SCORE	

What Your Score Really Means

Score: 9 - 15

You are physically active and have no major concerns about injury or soreness from exercising.

If you are looking for other ways to add in some new routines, you can access some of my favorite fitness routines here:
www.acceleratedmethod.com/movement

Score: 16 - 35
You probably do some type of physical activity during the week. It may even be working in the yard, or walking on your way to work, but you are out and about moving your body.

You could use some additional fitness routines to accelerate your weight loss and overall physique.

Working out is top of mind for you, but you may just be too busy to find the time to do it. I have some 24-minute (or less) exercises you can access here:
www.acceleratedmethod.com/movement

Score 36+
Working out is a challenge for you. You may be concerned about injury or pain by starting a new exercise regime.

You might think that to make any progress at all with your weight or strength, you need to spend hours at the gym working with a trainer.

You don't have the time or the energy to figure it out, and your motivation is so low right now that it's just not a priority to "get in shape."

Before you consider any change to your diet or exercise plans, I'd like you to focus on Chapter 11, which includes a section about mindset and understanding why change is so hard for us humans.

If you have been struggling with yo-yo dieting or the up-and-down weight loss before, first, implement the "first step" outlined below.

What to Start with Right Now:

- Pause for a moment and think about your previous attempts to get your health in order. You learned something about yourself in each one of them — even if it was what NOT to do! Let's learn from all those lessons so you don't repeat them. We want this health and fitness journey to be a blast, after all. And it CAN be! (It SHOULD be!) But first, let's get clear on what you like to do and what you don't. For example, you may have once taken a Crossfit class, or did a boot camp session where your ass got kicked so hard that you could barely walk for a week afterward. We don't want that! (And for the record, I would never let that happen to you.)

  So do this exercise right now: Get a legal pad and draw a line down the middle of the page. On the left side, make a list of all the things you DON'T like about exercising. Or things you don't want to do again. Or have no interest in doing. And then make a list on the right side of the page of all the things you WOULD enjoy doing. For example, if you hated that Crossfit class, then you might write the following down the left side of the page:

> *I hate being too sore the next day.*
>
> *I don't want some aggro bro-trainer yelling at me.*
>
> *I don't want to feel exhausted.*

Or if you loathed that bootcamp session you once had, then you might write:

> I don't want to do some crazy hardcore bootcamp where I'm laying my elbows in dog poop in some godforsaken field somewhere.

- And then going down the right side of the page, maybe your list would look like this:

  I don't like long distance running, but I might be okay with some short sprints.

  I'm okay with lifting weights, but I don't want to go to the gym to do it.

  Jumping rope seems like fun.

  I'm okay with long walks.

You get the idea. Remember, the above list is only a hypothetical!

Write a list that suits YOU. Again, the point here is just to get some much-needed clarity so that we can design you a program you'll actually stick with.

The point of *all* this is to meet you where you are. Then from there, we can design a plan you'll actually enjoy doing.

Roadblock #6: You're Totally Stressed Out

The biggest roadblock on this list: Stress.

It's no secret that excessive stress will rapidly deplete you mentally and physically. We all know this from experience. But it can be such an easy thing to dismiss, or we too often accept it as just "how life is."

But it doesn't have to be. Which is why we're going to do something about it. But first, let's understand what's really happening here.

Stress is not only a major factor in how you're feeling, it also negatively affects your musculoskeletal system, respiratory system, and gut health.

That means stress doesn't just make it harder for you to implement positive change in your life; it actually affects crucial areas of your physical health.

Consider the following:

- Stress increases muscle tension which causes headaches, back pain, neck stiffness, and more.
- Stress causes your breathing patterns to become more shallow which interrupts the flow of oxygen to your cells and the annexation of carbon dioxide.
- Stress also affects your gut where 70 percent of your immune system is housed. Illness, lack of energy, your bad mood, bloating/gas/irregular bowels, even

disrupted sleep start when stress wreaks havoc on your gut.

If there is anything you take away from this book, it's this: if you want to start feeling better quickly, focus on stress management.

Here's the problem: You know the warning signs of a stressed system, but then everyone just gives you the standard advice to just "stop stressing out" without really telling you HOW!

It's frustrating, (which adds even more stress)!

So let me give you a tremendous technique you can begin using immediately.

What to Start with Right Now:

Here's an incredible technique to reduce your stress levels *instantly.*

Don't dismiss this because it's so simple. It's quite powerful.

This was developed by the Navy SEALs, (so you know it's effective and bad-ass)! They utilize this breath technique to amplify concentration, sharpen mental acuity, and keep calm even in the most stressful of situations.

So, what is it?

It's called box breathing.

Box breathing is a guided breath technique to lower your stress levels, promote higher levels of focus and stimulate your parasympathetic nervous system, which essentially is your “rest and digest” process.

Doing this will lower your blood pressure, slow down your heart rate, and you’ll feel calmer instantly.

Here’s how to do it:

Sit comfortably in an upright position, feet flat on the floor. Rest your hands in your lap, and close your eyes.

For (approximately) a minute, breathe normally. (You overachievers will want to time it... just go with it.) Allow yourself to settle into the chair.

Drop your shoulders away from your ears and see if you can relax any tense muscles.

Exhale deeply.

Inhale slowly to the count of four. Hold your breath to the count of four. Exhale to the count of four.

Hold that to the count of four. Repeat four complete rounds.

You may feel lightheaded when you start using box breathing. If so, open your eyes and return to normal breathing. Don’t get up from the chair right away. Once you practice this more, your body will adjust.

Give it a try and experience the power of what effective breath work can do for you.

You should also know there are several variations to the traditional box breathing technique. These are important because each one will put you in a slightly different, heightened state of focus and calm. You can deploy these techniques based on the stressful situation you're about to enter or the amount of stress you're already experiencing.

I privately coach clients with this type of technique, and I can tell you it works wonders. I also have an entire toolkit of stress management techniques that I use with all of my clients. I tailor each one to whatever the client needs.

Let me also add this: Reducing your stress is something that everyone gives lip service to but that very few guys actually will follow up on because they're so used to "powering through." That's where accountability comes in, and it's what I offer inside my high-level coaching. To find out more, click here: *https://www.acceleratedmethod.com/call*

Remember, you also have several tools already outlined in the other roadblock sections. Start by implementing these as well.

Learn to say no, track your time and responsibilities, delegate what doesn't serve you, prioritize 30 minutes for yourself every day, get curious about your relationship with food, and learn about the stories you carry around with you from your past experiences.

I teach additional techniques in my Accelerated Method Program, but the action steps listed in this chapter are an excellent start. It was no accident that the No. 1 roadblock, stress, appears last on this list. Use the tools I've listed to reduce your stress and recapture your best life.

✔ Success Check-in Exercise

Before we proceed with the rest of the book, let's first check in with where you're at right now in your overall health.

Below, rate yourself on a scale from 1-5 on how accurate the statements are. 1 means "not accurate at all," and 5 means "most accurate."

Once you've rated yourself for each statement, total up your scores and then use the Answer Key to determine your next steps.

Success Check-In Statement	Self-Rating
I tend to push myself beyond my mental and physical limits.	
I often say, "When I get through (situation/event), then I'll take a day off."	

I fall asleep on the couch when I get home from work, and I need to take naps on the weekends to "catch up" on rest.	
I ignore signs that my body is giving me when I am feeling run down or unwell.	
If I knew what to do to "get better," I'd do it. I just don't know where to start.	
Taking time off or giving myself a break because I'm rundown makes me feel guilty.	
I avoid going to the doctor if I don't feel well.	
My schedule is non-stop and relentless, but I don't know how to change that.	
I'm eating on the go, and it's not the best food.	
I am constantly feeling the pull between work and family. I need to be in two places at once.	
I have often thought, "I'm sick and tired of being sick and tired."	

I know I could accomplish so much more in life if I only had more time and energy.	
TOTAL UP YOUR SCORE	

What Your Score Really Means

Score: 12 - 19

You are managing life and business well right now, but some warning lights are showing up, and chances are you are ignoring them because you still have everything "under control."

You may be thinking something like, "Phew, last week was a beast, but I'll get some rest this weekend and be fresh by Monday morning."

Or you may be noticing a few more aches and pains throughout your body, but play it off as "getting older."

Your work and life schedule feel intense, but you tell yourself that you can handle it all and push yourself more than usual.

Maybe you are starting to notice that you are staying up later to "decompress" after a busy day and find yourself snacking late at night because you didn't eat that much during the day.

Here's the truth. While everything feels intense but manageable, you will probably continue to push yourself more and more and keep easing yourself towards burnout.

This is the moment, (and the easiest moment), to start to create better habits for yourself so that you don't end up completely depleting yourself.

Read this book with an open mind. Treat the "first step" at the end of this section as your fundamentals to continually implement to keep your stress at a manageable level.

Score: 20 - 39

If your score is in this zone, you know that everything in your life is starting to overwhelm you. You can still do what you need to do every day in your professional and personal life, but you are feeling the effects of the constant juggle of it all.

You are likely finding yourself pushing through your days, looking forward to getting home, and collapsing on the couch so everything can slow down for a little bit.

Physically, you are not feeling like yourself at all. You are noticing the number on the scale creeping up and seeing deeper bags under your eyes. You may also notice that certain foods are bothering you now more than ever, and often, you struggle with indigestion and stomach discomfort.

You may also be noticing that your mood is a little less positive than before. You used to be able to "rally" and shift your mindset into a better state. Now, it may seem like you are putting on a "happy" face at work and home.

If you are in this zone, it's time to look at your schedule and sleep habits. These two areas are the simplest to fix but will have a big impact on your energy levels.

You may be able to recapture some more time for yourself if you can clear off your calendar and take some pressure and responsibilities off of your shoulders. By allowing yourself some more downtime and "you" time, you can hit the "reset button" on your day.

At this point, your sleep habits are probably being affected. The stress and the late nights are getting to you, and even though you are exhausted, you are having trouble winding down or shutting off.

Start with the first step outlined below, thirty minutes a day to yourself, and continue forward addressing the areas of sleep (Chapter 7), hormones (Chapter 5), and nutrition (Chapter 8) for more ways to address the stress present in your life.

Score: 40 - 60

You know that you have reached a point of depletion and frustration. You may be wondering how you got to this point and want to find ways to "feel better."

Mentally and physically, everything is off, and you have no idea what to deal with first, (and you just don't have the time or energy to figure it all out).

I know how you feel. This is the point I had reached as well, and it's not a good place to land.

Here's what I can tell you. The methods in this book can

help you get started. Doing any, (and hopefully all), of the recommendations in this book will make an impact on your life.

The very first place to start is getting your energy back.

If you are at this point, just take the first step. Don't try to change everything at once. Your mind and body will push back. Start small. Stay consistent, and you will see a positive change!

What to Start with Right Now:

- If you haven't already, put 30 minutes in your calendar every single day for you. You and only you. Treat it like an official meeting. What are you going to do with that time? Start with nothing! You heard me. If "doing nothing" sounds extreme, then I encourage you to use that time by going for a simple walk and putting your phone on airplane mode, (or don't take it with you at all). Going for a walk can do absolute wonders for your stress levels and can help improve overall mental clarity. It sounds silly, and I can already hear the 101 reasons you say you can't possibly find the time to do this, but I'm telling you right now- this is a real game changer. Try it for 30 straight days and tell me I'm wrong!

Key Chapter Takeaways

The Six Common Roadblocks:

- **Not Enough Time!** Are you controlling your day or is your day controlling you?
- **Not Enough Energy!** You're past the hustle and grind stage of your life. Now, it's time to work smarter and set up a holistically enjoyable existence.
- **Unsustainable Expectations.** You want to be a real man? One that shows up in all the areas of your life? Great. I'll help you get there without needing a catnap on the weekends.
- **You Struggle With Making Healthy Food Choices.** Need I say more? Your food will either fuel you or drain you.
- **Overcoming Past Injuries and Bad Experiences.** For some of my clients, a big concern is their past experience of being injured during these health attempts. I am here to help you create a sustainable, easily-repeatable lifestyle that starts exactly where you are and steps you into the life you want.
- **You're Totally Stressed Out.** The biggest roadblock on this list.

Addressing one of these roadblocks will help improve the others. They are all integrated in regards to your health and well-being. Each section contains an assessment and first steps I recommend you implement to start going from sick and tired to back on fire.

Here's the thing about improving all these areas: It can be simple, but it's not always easy! That's one reason I created my advanced level Accelerated Method coaching program. It's where I give you a totally customized plan of attack that's guaranteed to work for YOU. If you want to find out more about how I can personally help you "get the old you back" without having to take over your entire life in the process, then let's chat about it. Simply click the link below to schedule a call to chat:

https://www.acceleratedmethod.com/call

CASE STUDY

Brandon H., Utah, High-level Executive

"It truly has been life-changing and a transformation."

"I was working around the clock. 60, 70, 80 hours a week. Traveling just continually and not feeling great.

I went from my college years of being in the best shape of my life to progressing in my professional career and devoting all of my time to my professional career and anything else I had left towards my family.

In general, not spending time on me. Not focusing on me and my health.

Career-wise, things were going well but health-wise, not too great. I was putting on weight, not eating healthy, and not exercising because I always felt like I never had enough time. Not sleeping enough, being tired all the time.

Professionally, I've always been a fairly confident individual, but when you don't like what you see in the mirror it can take its toll on your confidence. So there's no doubt it was impacting my performance in the office as well, not to mention, my personal life.

For me, over the last couple of months since I got into the program, I've learned how to manage stress. And even though professionally things are crazier than they've ever been, I don't feel like I'm as stressed as I once was under less stressful circumstances professionally.

Life has been great. I feel better. I have more energy. I have energy until night, until after the kids go to bed. I feel like I never run out of energy, and I'm just getting started. I know that it's going to get even better. It truly has been life-changing and a transformation.

My family and loved ones comment all the time that I'm more positive and that they see a kind of pep in my step, so to speak. And professionally, I feel like my mental clarity is at an all-time high.

I feel great in the way that I'm managing our business and the way that I'm leading my team here at work, so it's been an amazing change for me.

Physically, I've lost about 34 pounds. I've lost crazy inches in my chest, my gut, my waist, my neck. I'm fitting into clothes that I haven't been able to wear for years.

And then sleep, that was a game-changer. That's made such a big difference which has led to some of the great results that I've made putting in the work for the last 60 days.

I've had so much more energy, so during the weekday and weekend I'm spending more quality time playing with the kids inside and outside, doing activities together.

As a result, I've become a much better family man. The best part about this program is it teaches you how to do it and not be a drastic time-suck."

— Brandon H., Utah, High-Level Executive

CHAPTER 4

What Is 'Health Debt' Really Costing You?

In the decade I've worked as a health coach to high-performing men over the age of 40, I've learned one crucial thing.

I want you to picture it like this:

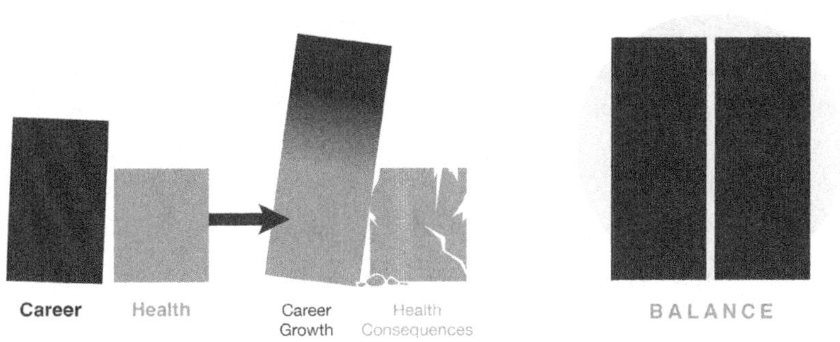

Two stacks of blocks. One represents the growth of his professional career, the other the growth of his personal life.

The guy that usually comes to me is successful and driven. The growth of his career stack is on point. Block after block after block stacks on top of each other. It's tough, but rewarding.

The second stack, his personal growth stack, gets less attention. If there is anything left in the tank after throwing down handfuls of blocks on the first stack, then maybe the second stack gets some movement, though it's never fully engaged.

Here's the problem. While this imbalance is unintentional, the lack of growth in the second stack causes the first stack to become overbalanced, and it all comes crashing down.

With both stacks of blocks scattered all over the floor, nothing feels right… or possible.

Pushing to new heights doesn't seem possible. All you seem to be able to do is juggle tasks. You struggle in maintenance mode. Instead of that feeling of satisfaction when accomplishing something great, you find nothing holds the same enjoyment anymore. The thrill is gone.

True story: One guy I worked with used to get off work and would randomly drive himself around for 30 minutes before going home because he didn't have the energy for his family. He needed that highway alone time for a reset. Otherwise, he'd feel like he was leaving one job to clock in at another. We sure do find some strange coping strategies, don't we?

Our society has ingrained in us a "work hard hero" mentality. And this is all well and good, but simply working hard can't last because the all-too-critical component in that equation is YOU. As soon as you collapse, so does everything else. So, far from being a luxury, taking care of that second stack of blocks — your health, well-being and mental state — is equally, if not *more* important, than building up that first stack.

If your career block collapses and your personal tower is strong, then you can turn around, start again, rebuild and power up, no matter what.

However, if that second block collapses ... well, then *everything* stops.

Never forget that you are your number one asset. You are also your number one liability.

Let me show you how this plays out, and what can be done about it.

Are You In Health Debt?

Another guy I worked with received a heart-wrenching question from his daughter one day.

Brian was a lawyer with an intense lifestyle- he was close to burnout and exhaustion. He endured brutal workdays scheduled down to the minute and was continually pulled in a million directions.

He was aware that his health was declining, but he couldn't find the time to figure out what to do about it.

Brian's life had become transactional. And the question that flew from his daughter's mouth that day summed it all up in just twelve gut-wrenching words:

"Daddy, if I give you a paycheck, will you play with me?"

Ooof.

When we first spoke, I asked Brian one simple question that changed everything.

"How much do you think you're losing in actual dollars by not taking control of your health and life?"

There was a long pause on the other end of the phone.

This is a concept I call "Health Debt." Brian had never thought about it that way. In fact, most guys I work with have never calculated their life in this way.

Let's take a look. Here is how you calculate your Health Debt.

1. Determine how much you earn in an average hour, (whether your rate is hourly, salary, or project).
2. Ask yourself, on a scale of 1-10, where are your energy levels? (1 being nothing and 10 being peak performance). Now translate that energy level into hours lost each week.
3. Multiply your "hours lost each week" by the average amount you earn in an hour.

Let's get back to this client.

Brian was a lawyer charging $1,000/hour, (yes, that's his hourly rate), and averaged a 60-70 hour workweek.

Between hitting snooze on the alarm clock several times, taking extra trips to grab coffee, taking catch-up naps in the early evening and on the weekends, and battling lack of concentration and a foggy brain during work time, he labeled his energy levels at about a 4 or a 5.

Estimating about 10 lost hours of work time each week, here's what that looks like:

$1000 x 10 hours = $10,000 a week!

There are three major issues going on here:

1. Brian's stress levels were through the roof, and he was constantly chasing time. He had no clue where to start to get the upper hand on this situation.

2. He was "working" 60-70 hours a week, but losing money because no work was getting done. No small amount of time was spent just trying to get his head in the game.

3. He was missing out on precious family time because of work, where, (don't forget), nothing was getting done.

He was stuck in a terrible cycle, and one I see too many high-achieving top performers experience. This is what drives most clients to the point of radical change.

You probably don't realize how much time is wasted in your day due to fatigue, stress, anxiety or whatever else you might be suffering from.

What's worse, you might think you're sacrificing things like health and relationships for your professional development, which you justify as being for "the greater good"... but is it, really?

Taking a look at your Health Debt will clue you in to the following reality: When your physical and mental health is depleted, everything suffers.

Now, you may think to yourself:

"I make the same amount of money no matter how crappy I may feel."

Yeah, you might make the same amount of money, but what else is this costing you?

And even if that is true, even if you make the same amount no matter how good or crappy you feel, is that the sort of life you want to live, just half-assing it, not really caring how you feel? Yes, the money is a worthy factor to consider, but what about your PRIDE? What about the kind of life you want to live? Think about being an example for your kids or those you lead at work. Don't you want to be efficient? Isn't that why you're reading this book in the first place? Because you aspire for more?

Regardless, no matter what your situation is right now, use the steps below to calculate your health debt and consider what it's costing you.

Then we're going to turn this health debt into a health *surplus* as we go through this book.

Here's What to Start with Right Now:

To improve your productivity and overall well-being and reduce your health debt, follow these steps:

1. Determine your average hourly earnings, either by your hourly rate, salary, or project. If you don't calculate your earnings per hour, estimate a number based on your total salary or project.

2. On a legal pad, write down the days of the week you work. Under each day, divide the day into four time blocks: morning, late morning, afternoon, and evening.

3. For each time block, rate your energy levels on a scale of 1-10, with 1 being low and 10 being high.

4. Calculate the total number of hours lost each week by multiplying your energy level for each time block by the number of hours in that block. For example, if your energy level is 3 in the morning, and you consider the morning to be 3 hours long, you have lost 3 x 3 = 9 hours of productivity for that time block.

5. Multiply your "hours lost each week" by your average hourly earnings to get your total health debt.

6. Look for patterns in your energy levels over the four time blocks. Are there certain times of day when your energy is consistently high or low? What could you do to reduce the health debt during those times?

Remember, the goal of this exercise is to become aware of your energy levels and health debt, not to criticize yourself! By understanding your current energy levels and health debt, you can follow the steps within this book to create a health surplus and improve your productivity and well-being.

Key Chapter Takeaways

- Your life is like two stacks of blocks.

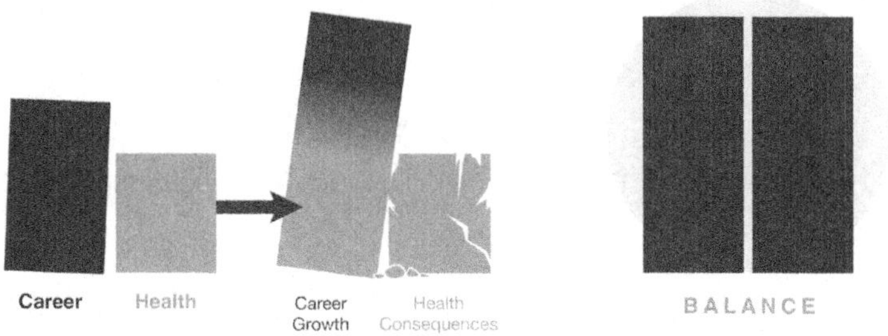

Imbalance between these two stacks is what causes a crash and burnout.

- You are your number one asset and also your number one liability.
- Calculate your health debt, [average hourly rate x hours lost each week = health debt].

CASE STUDY

Paul C., South Carolina, Real Estate Professional

"I've lost 50 pounds. I've lost 8 inches in my waist, and I wear a size 30 now. I have energy to do things that I could never do before."

"I was always exhausted, working all the time, trying to deal with family and kids. Had no energy. I was overweight, tired. My second child was just born, work was awesome, I was busier than ever, but there was something missing. I didn't realize how much making health changes in my life would change all aspects. In doing this, I was able to be so much more focused and felt so much better that I think it came out in a lot of areas. I mean, I was able to improve my customer service scores at work. I was able to improve sales at work and I continue to be the sales leader.

It used to be I would stay and have to work late all the time just to get things accomplished. But now, starting off my day focused, allows me to come into the office and do more in a shorter period of time. It's been one of those things that's proven that I can do anything that I want to do.

Over the course of my journey I've lost 50 pounds. I've lost 8 inches in my waist, and I wear a size 30 now. I have energy to do things that I could never do before. I mean, I can pick my kids up and toss them in the air and have fun and play and run and swim and jump. So there's just so many things that I can do physically that I couldn't do before."

— Paul C., South Carolina, Real Estate Professional

CHAPTER 5

Two Hidden Truths That Are Keeping You Sick and Tired

Let's get real for a minute. What used to work for you doesn't anymore.

I'm guessing that's one key driver that led to you picking up this book.

Oh sure, we dance around it in our normal, everyday conversations. We say things like:

"Well, I'm just getting older, that's all."

"My bones are aching — I'm certainly not 25 anymore, I'll tell you that!"

"Happens to everyone, right?"

HELL NO. It doesn't happen this way for everyone.

And look, it's perfectly fine if you have slid into the gradual decline that led you here.

It does indeed happen to a LOT of guys. (Maybe even the majority)!

There's no shame in it. The only shame would be to give in to it.

Here's what I know from deep in my bones and from working with hundreds of guys just like you: You DON'T have to accept feeling like crap as "inevitable."

It's *not* inevitable. And the even better news is, ***it can be reversed.***

This chapter will show you exactly how.

I'm about to share two hidden truths you may not know that have everything to do with your weight, energy, and mental health. They are the reasons why your previous attempts haven't gotten you clear-cut results.

Most health programs out there don't take either of these truths into consideration. It's why they peddle the hustle and grind mentality like a bad song on repeat.

When you work with me, these truths are the core foundation for every client I work with.

Let's get started.

Hidden Truth #1: Hormones (Yes, men have them, too)

First of all, as men age, there are several physical changes that commonly happen. One is the development of a "middle-aged spread."

You've heard of that, right? It's the tendency to gain weight around your midsection. Whether you refer to it as a beer belly or your "Dad Bod," let me be straight about one thing:

It's not a joke. There's nothing to love about love handles. It's actually a deadly serious issue, and I'm about to explain why.

I'm sorry to be such a buzz-kill, but excess body fat is a major risk factor for all manner of cardiovascular disease, strokes, and a host of other health problems.

But let's talk about WHY. This is crucial to know before you go about solving it.

So weight gain is often due to a combination of factors, including a slowing metabolism, decreased muscle mass, and changes in hormone levels.

These changes can make it harder for men to regain the energy they had in their twenties. But that's just the start. It also makes it harder to burn calories and do all the right things to help your body operate the way it was designed to. It messes with your appetite, gives you late-night cravings for Twinkies, and can even affect your performance, ahem, "down there," (a lower sex drive combined with a difficulty to get and maintain an erection).

It's all about hormones. This is what almost no one talks about.

One such hormone is testosterone, which you've surely heard about a thousand times, but what you might *not* know is how it helps regulate muscle mass and body fat distribution.

I'll get into this briefly. This is important, and it won't hurt a bit, I promise.

As men age, testosterone levels naturally begin to decline, which can lead to a loss of muscle mass and an increase in body fat, particularly around the midsection. (This decline can be slowed and even reversed.)

The age-related decline in testosterone can also sap your energy levels. (Two o'clock afternoon crash, we're looking at you, bud.) This happens for several reasons, including a reduced production of ATP, (a molecule that provides energy to cells), in the mitochondria, and age-related insulin resistance.

Ah, yes, insulin. I know you've heard about this, too. Insulin is a hormone that helps control your body's blood sugar level and metabolism, which is the process that turns the food you eat into energy.

Insulin by itself is not a problem. *But insulin resistance is.* This occurs when the body's cells don't respond as well to insulin, which can lead to high blood sugar levels and fatigue.

Insulin resistance is a massive factor in middle aged decline. It's the reason some guys, (and women, too, of course), can literally eat their way into developing Type 2 diabetes. And if you don't already know it, Type 2 diabetes is a greased chute into a host of catastrophes you *don't* ever want, such as heart disease, kidney disease, stroke, not to mention the possibility of serious damage to parts of your body like your eyes, limbs, and feet.

Belly fat is closely related to insulin resistance. And yes, the risk of developing insulin resistance increases as you get older. But again, the good news is that it can be prevented with some pretty simple steps, (more on that shortly).

So let's talk about estrogen next. You may think of it as "the female hormone," but it's also essential for men. However, when estrogen levels increase in men, it leads to weight gain and a decrease in muscle mass.

You know how some men develop "man boobs?" While those have a variety of causes and aren't caused simply by rising levels of estrogen, they are very much related to a hormonal imbalance — the type of hormonal imbalance that this chapter can help you solve. (And why it's a central focus of my work with private clients because it's such a foundational game-changer.)

Finally, let's talk about the stress hormone cortisol.

It's not an exaggeration to say that cortisol is another silent killer of men. Of course, at the very least, it also contributes to a decrease in energy and weight gain.

Cortisol is produced any time you feel stress. This can lead to an increase in appetite and cravings for all manner of desserts, junk food and any other fat bomb treat that will have you looking for more holes on your belt.

Belly fat loves cortisol.

Cortisol can also interfere with the body's ability to regulate blood sugar levels which can lead to feelings of fatigue and low energy. It can also disrupt the body's natural sleep-wake cycle. If you've ever had a hard time falling asleep, or you wake up at 3 a.m. and have trouble getting back to sleep, then cortisol could be to blame. All of which, of course, will lower your energy even further.

And that's another thing you should know: Hormonal imbalances create a cascade of negative effects that affect your entire physical and mental well-being. They create a vicious cycle that makes it almost impossible to lose belly fat and power through your day with high energy.

Again, it's all so fixable! (And yes, we're getting to that shortly.)

So, what else is responsible for the dreaded middle aged spread other than hormones?

These: a sedentary lifestyle, poor diet, and excessive alcohol consumption.

In layman's terms, it means this: being a couch potato, eating like crap, and too much booze.

Let's take these one by one:

A sedentary lifestyle. Not enough exercise decreases your muscle mass and promotes weight gain. 'Nuff said, you already know this. I design customized workouts for my private clients to fit them, (and you'll see my general recommendations at the end of this chapter).

A poor diet. A diet high in calories, unhealthy fats, and refined carbohydrates can also contribute to weight gain. These types of foods are often high in empty calories and can easily lead to weight gain. In contrast, a diet rich in vegetables, fruits, healthy fats, and lean proteins can not only get you back to your ideal weight, but they're totally satisfying because they're nutritionally dense. They also give you a satisfying sense of being full, which blunts cravings for all the bad stuff. (Again, this is something I customize for my private clients, and you'll also see my general recommendations in this book.)

Excessive alcohol consumption. Anything more than moderate amounts of alcohol are devastating to the body. They don't call it a "beer belly" for nothing! And don't kid yourself, the hard stuff wreaks the same havoc on your organs and overall physical and mental health.

So now that we know what's causing the "middle aged spread," how do we fix it?

In just a minute, I'll give you some simple tips to begin addressing — even *reversing* — this dreaded condition.

I'm excited for you because I'll say it again: Physical, mental, and emotional decline after 40 is NOT inevitable!

But here's the problem: So many of the supposed solutions not only don't work to fix your hormones, but they can be flat-out dangerous.

Here's a partial list of things many guys do that DON'T work for high-performing men over 40:

Personal trainers who insist on putting you in "beast mode," forcing you into workouts that are unnecessarily brutal, no fun whatsoever, or even flat-out dangerous

Chronic Cardio, aka "running it off," "living on the treadmill" or "grinding it out" on expensive machines like

NordicTrack or Peloton

Franchise cardio gyms that have turned chronic cardio into a business model ... but suck up too much of your time without delivering the results you need

Hardcore bootcamps (just more beast mode, except with a military feel)

Crash or starvation dieting (which never works long term and never will)

Extreme diets such as keto and HCG

"Fat burning and energy-boosting" supplements that aren't much more than expensive caffeine

CrossFit, which can often lead to injuries and is rarely sustainable anyway

Brutalizing and Boring Home Workout Programs such as P90X and Insanity

Josh's Story

My client Josh is a good example of what can happen when you try the wrong things or when you think you're taking a step in the right direction... but it actually only makes the problem *worse*.

Josh was like a lot of my clients when he came to see me: tired, heavier than he wanted to be, feeling like crap, and trapped in a life he didn't want or even recognize anymore.

In the past, Josh was like a lot of guys whenever he found himself packing on some extra pounds. He would go on a crash diet, skip meals, and do some running.

Hey, in your twenties, this can actually work in the short term. It can even work somewhat into your thirties. (But it's still not good for you — please don't get the impression I recommend this approach for anyone of any age.)

But once you hit 40? Forget about it! It's a whole different ball game.

Josh found this out the hard way. None of his quick-hit, smoke-and-mirrors strategies worked for him anymore.

He began to panic a little because what used to work wasn't anymore. Here's how Josh described it to me:

"Right around the time I turned 40, I wasn't able to drop a few pounds by running every now and then. I wasn't able to do that anymore. So the frustration started adding up. I couldn't do a crash diet real quick and run around the block a few times for a couple of weeks and solve my problems. Those tricks were not working anymore. I got frustrated and mad. And I didn't know what I was going to do."

So Josh did what a lot of guys would do. He joined a gym and hired a personal trainer.

Smart move, right?

Well, it CAN be. But it can also be a nightmare if you're

paired with someone who doesn't truly understand your situation.

This happens a lot more than you might guess. I've seen this countless times with clients before they find me.

What happened with Josh was common. They paired him with a trainer who was shredded and ripped ... who then put Josh through a training regimen so over-the-top hard core that Josh never wanted to lift another weight again.

"I was like, this is what you do, right?" Josh said. "This is how you achieve happiness in life: You show up at the gym at six o'clock, and you work out super hard. I'm doing jump squats with this beast mode trainer at six in the morning who's 23. And I'm 40. And from day one, I threw up in the bathroom. I was miserable. I did that a few times. And I'm just like, this is hell, this can't be the way to sustainability. And it wasn't for me. Within a few weeks, I stopped showing up and disappeared. I went back to my own routines of running and skipping meals and not sleeping and just crazy stuff."

That's when Josh came to me. I designed him a sustainable transformation program that not only delivered results, but was *enjoyable*, something he would actually look forward to. I'm happy to report that Josh met his goals and continues to do well.

So let's talk more about what DOES work.

You need to find ways to naturally balance your hormones. Period, full stop.

'The Blue Screen of Death'

Let me close this section on hormones with an analogy that might be helpful.

Remember back in the day with old computers, when they would crash all the time giving you that "blue screen of death?"

It would become impossible to complete any work or get anything done!

Well, you should think of your hormones in a similar way. When your hormones are out of whack, you have a metabolic profile that's stuck. Just like the Blue Screen of Death where nothing works, it becomes extremely difficult to drop belly fat and increase your energy for the long term.

However, fixing your hormones reboots everything. It's like giving yourself a brand new operating system.

Let me give you some tips to get started.

Here's What to Start With Right Now:

1. **Exercise and Daily Movement:** Just 15-30 minutes of daily movement will support healthy hormone production. In Chapter 6, I give you a simple movement routine you can use to start your day. If you're interested in getting a more customized routine that fully takes into account your schedule, your current fitness level, including any preexisting conditions or injuries, and incorporates activities you

actually *like* to do, then I invite you to visit: *https://www.acceleratedmethod.com/call* to schedule a call with me or one of my team members. This is part of a complete plan I give all my high-level coaching clients.

2. **Eat More Protein Dense, Healthy Fat, and Fibrous Based Meals:** Increase the amount of nutrient dense foods you are eating, (unprocessed, natural foods), and have a balanced intake of lean protein, healthy fat, and fibrous based meals.

3. **Manage Your Stress:** Excessive amounts of stress are wreaking havoc on your hormones and your entire system. The bad news is, even if you eat clean and exercise regularly, if you don't find a way to limit your stress, you'll stay stuck and frustrated.

   These four final action steps will help you start dialing down your stress levels:

4. **Get a Restful Night's Sleep:** Quality sleep is vital in balancing your hormones. Yeah, yeah, I know you've heard before how important sleep is. *But it really, really is!* This is one of those profoundly impactful factors that makes everything go better. And yes, I know you're busy with 101 other things. But you simply must find a way to get at least seven quality hours of uninterrupted sleep a majority of your nights, or you'll remain sick and tired.

5. **Get Outside:** Fresh air and the Vitamin D from sunshine help boost your testosterone levels. It's also a great way to lower your stress levels. This

is another one of those simple-but-profound truths we all know but is too easily dismissed. Take just a 10-minute walk twice a day and tell me you don't feel an immediate difference!

6. **Supplements that Support Hormones:** There are several supplements which can help balance your hormones — as well as a few important ones I recommend to my private clients, depending on the needs of each — but one of my top recommendations is *Ashwagandha.** A scientific study found it to be beneficial for reducing inflammation, boosting muscle strength, improving brain function, and increasing testosterone levels.

   **As with all recommended supplements, please check with your doctor first*

7. **Joy, Laughter, Happiness:** The science doesn't lie: Countless studies show that doing activities you enjoy, having fun, laughing with loved ones, and having a sense of gratitude can enormously impact how you feel both mentally and physically. Start looking for opportunities to take little "exit ramps" from whatever is going on throughout your day to milk a little more laughter and joy. (It's okay, you can get back to work as soon as you want!)

Hidden Truth #2: Inflammation (It's worse than you know)

You've heard the word "inflammation" a thousand times, and you probably know it's a bad thing.

But here's something you might not know: Inflammation actually serves an incredibly valuable purpose in the body and is quite a GOOD thing in certain situations.

It's important to know the difference, so I'll explain briefly.

Inflammation is a natural process in which your body protects itself from infections caused by bacteria or viruses. It's also your body's necessary response when you suffer an injury, such as a cut or wound.

And that's great. You *want* your body to have an inflammatory response when it's facing an invader, or when it's been injured.

So when is inflammation a bad thing? It's when inflammation becomes a *chronic* response, triggered when your body is facing no outside danger. That becomes a huge problem.

This can happen when you have a weakened or compromised immune system. In that case, your body triggers an inflammatory response- even when there is *nothing* to protect against. And that's NOT good. That's when white blood cells may begin attacking healthy tissue and organs, causing even more inflammation- which can affect processes throughout the body.

That's the type of inflammation you need to guard against. So, what causes chronic inflammation, and how do you know when you have it?

First, let's determine whether this is a problem for you in the first place.

Here are some symptoms you may experience if you have chronic inflammation:

- Body pain
- Low energy
- Constant fatigue
- Depression, anxiety, and other mood disorders
- Gastrointestinal issues, such as constipation, diarrhea, or acid reflux
- Weight gain
- Frequent infections and sickness

Do any of those sound familiar? If so, you could have a problem with chronic inflammation.

Before we get into how to fix inflammation, let's first look at how it starts in the first place. These are the most important, high-level causes of inflammation you need to be aware of:

(A few of these were mentioned earlier. They're worth repeating because they're too easily overlooked by many.)

- **Chronic stress.** Stress leads to elevated levels of cortisol, which is also linked to increased abdominal fat. *No bueno* for obvious reasons!
- **Alcohol.** Excessive alcohol consumption can lead to chronic inflammation.
- **Smoking.** No surprise, right? Smoking increases

inflammation in the body by causing accumulation of various inflammation-promoting bacteria.

- **Poor diet.** A diet that is high in processed, refined foods and low in vegetables and other high quality nutrients can contribute to chronic inflammation.
- **Nutritional deficiencies.** Any nutrient deficiency can lead to cellular damage either directly or indirectly, but some are primarily known to cause inflammation, including low levels of Vitamin D, Vitamin B6, and Vitamin B12. I love this reason because it's something so easily fixed.
- **Lack of consistent exercise.** A sedentary lifestyle can contribute to chronic inflammation.
- **Obesity.** Excess weight can also increase inflammation as it can place stress on the body that leads to additional cellular damage.

I expect that you saw yourself in this chapter somewhere.

By far, the biggest complaints I get from my clients when they come to me are these: tiredness, fatigue, lethargy, and weight gain. They're all abetted by the above factors and made worse by imbalanced hormones and inflammation.

Not fully understanding your hormones, or the role of inflammation, has likely contributed to your current state of being. It's now my job to help you gain the education and form the right action plan to find your way out.

What to Start with Right Now

The first step to reducing inflammation in the body: Follow a healthy nutrition protocol and reduce your intake of inflammatory and acidic foods such as processed foods, fried foods, and refined carbohydrates, including sugar.

Look, if you've been on a fast-food-all-American diet, this might sound like a massive change in your eating habits, but in the grand scheme of things, it actually isn't. The key is to have a sincere desire to change and to simply get started.

Start by doing the following:

- **Stop eating fast food.** If that's too big of an ask, then cut your frequency in half. For instance, if you currently eat fast food, say, four times per week, then cut it back to two.
- **Keep a stash in your car of some alternative healthy foods** like a bag of almonds or mixed nuts.
- **Stop mindless snacking.** Here's how: First, drink plenty of water. Believe it or not, sometimes your body confuses thirst for hunger. Drinking water can help to curb your appetite and prevent mindless snacking. So keep a bottle of water with you wherever you go, and you might be amazed how it prevents you from even thinking about eating.
- **Keep unhealthy snacks out of reach.** If you don't have easy access to unhealthy snacks, you'll be less likely to eat them. Sounds obvious, but it really works!

- **Practice mindfulness when eating.** Really pay attention to your food and how it tastes, rather than eating while distracted. This can help you be more aware of when you are full, and it will become easier to stop eating.

- **Notice what sort of mood or emotion you're feeling when you feel the urge to hit a drive-in fast food joint.** Then plan for an alternative behavior for the next time you feel that urge. For example, let's say that you often find yourself craving fast food when you're feeling stressed or overwhelmed. The next time you start to feel that urge, take a moment to pause and check in with yourself. Ask yourself, "What am I actually feeling right now? Am I feeling stressed or overwhelmed? Is it fear? Worry?" Whatever it is, identify it. (If you're not used to doing this, it will be good practice because identifying what you're feeling in the moment is a key step in being able to stop self-destructive behaviors.)

  Once you've identified the emotion you're experiencing, come up with a replacement behavior rather than going to a fast food restaurant. For example, you might go for a walk to clear your head, call a friend to chat, or simply drink some water. Will it be as fun as hitting the fast-food drive-in? Probably not! But hang in there and stay with it. Pretty soon it will become second nature, and you will have made a huge stride in improving your situation.

Bottom line: By noticing the emotion you're feeling and coming up with an alternative behavior, you can learn to cope with your emotions in a healthy way and reduce the likelihood of turning to fast food as a coping mechanism.

My 'Accelerated Method' rebalances hormones and reboots your metabolism, allowing you to now drop fat and increase your energy levels *naturally*, like someone in their early 20's.

To be honest, this entire business of rebalancing your hormones and metabolism is the secret to how we have successfully helped hundreds of high performers get back to that "bounce out bed energy" they had back in their early 20's. It also lets them shed extra pounds, skyrocket energy levels, and pretty soon, they're wearing whatever they want with a newfound confidence.

We're able to do this because we can dial in each client's protocol based on what will work for *them*. (Everyone is different.) If you'd like to find out more about this, please visit: https://www.acceleratedmethod.com/call and schedule a call with us.

Key Chapter Takeaways

There are two hidden truths that will derail any health plan you're on if you don't take them into account:

- **Hormones.** Understand how low testosterone, insulin resistance, and cortisol can wreak havoc on your health and nullify your best intentions.

  Realize that chronic stress, lack of sleep, and a poor diet will significantly crash your energy levels and sabotage your overall wellness. The good news is there are ways to naturally balance these hormones and doing so will bring a relatively quick turnaround in how you feel. Follow the tips in this chapter to make that happen.

- **Inflammation:** Understand what chronic inflammation is and the key role it plays in creating constant fatigue, depression, anxiety, gastrointestinal issues, weight gain, and sickness.

  By following a healthy nutrition protocol full of anti-inflammatory foods, you'll be taking an important step in combating chronic inflammation.You can do this by reducing your intake of inflammatory and acidic foods such as processed foods, fried foods, and refined carbohydrates, including sugar. I cover all of this in Part 2 of this book.

CASE STUDY

Will S., Virginia, Senior Engineer

"Now, I have more energy and I have the ability to be at my desk at 7:30 and be ready to work and make good decisions and get so much more done by noon than I had done in a day or two days prior."

"I didn't feel too good. I was getting through the days with a struggle, waking up pretty lethargically hit and miss in the morning. I would get walks in but just not enough real exercise or any "me time" to be able to have the energy to tackle the day. The couch became my resting spot at the end of the day, and the weight came on.

And as the weight went on, the ability to exercise went way down, and my energy levels went down, I was able to function but just not quite in a clear and energetic state. It was the worst I had ever felt and the most I had ever weighed.

I weighed in one day, somewhere in the 250s. And, you know, it was just alarming. I went to the doctor for other reasons, and the doctor weighed me and asked me what football team I played for at that weight- which was a joke, of course, but just a reminder that, "Hey, you're really in a zone that you should not be in if you want to maintain some kind of healthy lifestyle."

Now, I have more energy and I have the ability to be at my desk at 7:30 and be ready to work and make good decisions and get so much more done by noon than I had done in a day or two days prior. No longer am I coming home and just going right to the couch, grabbing a beer or a cocktail, and just saying, "Hey, you deserve this, what a day."

So the physical results: I was once 250 and I think my waist was a 45, which was also pretty alarming. And then, as of this morning, I was 223.4 pounds and I've lost about three and a half inches off the waist. My favorite thing is being able to be cognizant and present in the morning after taking care of myself first and being able to deliver to others, myself, and my family much better for the rest of the day."

— Will S., Virginia, Senior Engineer

PART 2

Finding the Fire Within: The Path to Restored Health

CHAPTER 6

The Oxygen Mask Protocol

The guys I personally work with tell me the same thing every time: They're super successful with the weight of the world on their shoulders trying to balance everything.

And they always tell me how guilty they feel after a long day of work putting out fires and attending to everybody else.

They just don't have anything left in the tank to give.

It's not that they aren't excited to see their family. It's just that they're absolutely wiped out.

They can't engage with their partners. They can't go out in the yard and play with their kids. They make up excuses to get out of social events even if they want to go. There's not enough energy left for anything outside of work.

I get it. I've been there.

It's very easy for high-performing guys to want to put their work first. It's ingrained in us, right? We're instinctual *providers.* It's who we ARE. Which is why it feels so natural and effortless to forget about ourselves.

But it's the road to disaster. Which is why I always include my "Oxygen Mask Protocol" when working with high performers in their forties.

What is it? Well, as you've probably already guessed, it stems from the same thing you hear on every flight: Put on your own oxygen mask first.

The same thing holds true in your own life. But I know how easy it is to unknowingly disregard it. In fact, this is another one of those simple things we talked about back in Chapter 4: Easy to hear, harder to implement day in and day out.

Put aside any societal notions about selfishness and burn this into your brain right now:

The greatest gift you can give to anyone, your significant other, kids, employees, colleagues is your own happiness.

Think about that. If you're happy, what happens in each of those relationships?

You show up as a better, whole person. You're attentive, patient, and a strong decision-maker. When you are happy, you show up as the very best version of yourself, the one that you and others expect.

It's not selfish. It's actually the best gift you can give to those around you.

From my experience, one of the best ways to achieve happiness is to apply the 80/20 rule to the priorities in your life.

Here's what I mean: 20 percent of the effort you exert in your life yields 80 percent of your reality. In other words, 80 percent of your life will take care of itself if you focus your effort on the right 20 percent.

Putting on your own oxygen mask falls squarely in that all-important 20 percent.

Which is why my Oxygen Mask Protocol is so important.

All the various roles in life — provider, protector, rescuer — happen naturally once your oxygen mask is securely tightened. You simply can't be in those roles if it's not.

If you're burning the candle at both ends, putting on your oxygen mask first is the only solution.

Controlling your time and protecting your energy and confidence are two things I set up for all of my clients. One way we do that is by setting your day up to WIN with a strong morning routine.

This goes back to what we discussed in Chapter 3. Put yourself first for 30 minutes before anybody else wants your attention.

Here's what my client, Dusty, had to say about his morning routine:

"

> *"Every minute that I focus on myself first thing in the morning, it buys me two minutes inside the rest of my day. The amount of things that I accomplish in my workday now are far and*

beyond what I used to be capable of. And then I leave work at the end of the day, and I'm not exhausted. I feel like doing something else, starting another activity. I've learned that I don't have time not to do what I'm doing."

- Dusty G.
High-Level Executive & Business Owner

THAT'S the power of a great morning routine.

Morning routines are vital to your physical and mental health.

Now, don't worry, I'm not suggesting you do one of those morning routines where you work out for two hours, and journal your life away. Those things aren't bad, but my clients don't have time for that stuff.

Which means you don't either.

Before you even think about having a pot of coffee or a caffeine-pick-me-up tomorrow morning, try this instead...

The Oxygen Mask Protocol

Phase 1: The Morning Blackout

The morning blackout is a ritual that ensures you get YOU in first before anyone or anything wants your attention. The first thing you should do is either turn OFF your devices, or at least put them in airplane mode. I know this might feel difficult at first, but you can do it, trust me! (And the world will keep spinning on its axis, too.)

Phase 2: Hyper Hydrate

Here's what to do as soon as you wake up:

- Pour yourself one full liter of water (32 ounces), room temperature if possible.
- Squeeze one fourth to a half a lemon in there.
- Add a little pinch of pink Himalayan salt (about one teaspoon)
- Drink it down!

Yes, I fully realize I just handed you one of the simplest, most ordinary tips you could ever hear.

But it's also one of the most profound. I'm not kidding. The number of positive benefits that immediately start cascading throughout your body and mind when you take the time to do this, (and honestly, we're talking about less than one minute here), is truly staggering.

You will feel the benefits *immediately.*

It will boost your metabolism.

It will flush out toxins.

It will ease aches and pains.

It will give you a clearer complexion and more radiant skin.

It will help mitigate any sort of afternoon energy crash you might still be experiencing, (but shouldn't if you incorporate the suggestions in this book).

All that from a tall glass of water?

YES.

(And yes, of course, you'll want to continue hydrating throughout the day.)

So you might be wondering — why do we add the lemon and Himalayan pink salt?

It's because not only will the water rehydrate you, but the lemon will help protect and boost your immune system, and the Vitamin C will help you maintain a healthy weight.

The pink Himalayan salt will help your adrenal glands from burning out later on in the day. This is a type of rock salt that comes from the Himalayan Mountains. It is different from regular table salt because it is not refined and has not had its minerals removed. Instead, it contains 84 trace minerals that can be beneficial for the body.

Consuming pink Himalayan salt can offer a range of health benefits, including reducing muscle pain and cramping, improving sleep, aiding in digestion, balancing pH levels, boosting the immune system, aiding in weight loss, improving the appearance of skin, and providing relief during allergy season.

Still skeptical this is a difference-maker?

Then listen to what happened to Ben, a high-level executive who had racked up some impressive wins as a participant in my Accelerated Method coaching program. Along with losing close to 20 pounds, boosting energy to record levels, and becoming more mentally clear than he had in years, Ben told me something I found particularly interesting.

"Logan. I gotta tell ya, man, ever since starting this program, I no longer need to take Ibuprofen."

I asked him to elaborate.

"Before using your methodology, I felt like crap all the time. Popping Ibuprofen like it was going out of style. But I've gotten to the point where I no longer need to take it."

"What do you think is responsible for that?" I asked him.

He told me it was from learning how to hydrate. It was all from drinking more water.

"Hydration, really?" I said. "That's all it took?"

"Yeah. By tracking my intake, I realized I was hardly drinking any water. Once I started drinking more water, much of the pain I was experiencing went away."

This actually didn't surprise me. I've heard this often from many clients. Fact is, when it comes to functioning at optimal levels, adequate hydration is one of the most effective yet most overlooked solutions.

Don't dismiss this.

Failing to properly hydrate can negatively impact your physical and mental well-being ... *dramatically.*

Little hinges swing big doors. Our bodies are 50 to 70 percent water. Drinking an adequate amount of water is crucial if we want our cells and organs to function the way they should.

Water is crucial to many bodily functions, such as distributing nutrients, removing waste, and protecting and cushioning joints.

Even mild dehydration can cause a decrease in cognitive functioning.

Studies show that more than 70 percent of us are chronically dehydrated.

Being even moderately dehydrated by just 2 percent will lead to brain fog, a decrease in working memory, headaches, an increase in anxiety, and even emotional dips during the day.

Here's what's so exciting about performing this super-simple routine of drinking water first thing every morning: It has a much bigger impact than you would ever expect!

Seriously, if you give this routine a try for just seven days, you'll know what I mean.

There's another scientific piece to this that's fascinating. It has to do with the effects of water and caffeine. I'm going to explain this briefly, and then tell me you won't feel motivated instantly to give this daily water routine a try ...

So here's what happens after you go to bed ...

Your cells get dehydrated throughout the night, and most people wake up and choose a quick pick-me-up — coffee — that actually dehydrates them even more.

Not to mention, consuming any kind of caffeinated beverage the moment you wake up hinders your body's cortisol production, making it challenging for your body to wake up naturally.

Cortisol, you'll remember, is a hormone produced by the adrenal gland that plays a number of important roles in the body. And while it's true that high levels of cortisol can have negative effects on the body, it is also important to have some level of cortisol production in the morning. It helps wake up the body and start the day.

Cortisol levels reach their peak around 8 a.m. to 9 a.m. However, if you reach for that cup of joe as soon as you get out of bed, you'll interfere with the body's natural production of cortisol and disrupt the body's sleep-wake cycle. This is one big reason you feel fatigued in the afternoon.

The good news is that this is easily fixed. How? Simply by waiting an hour or two before you have that first cup of caffeine. That's it!

Will it be hard to *not* have coffee first thing in the morning if that's what you're used to? Perhaps. However, I encourage you to push through that and commit to trying it for 30 days before you judge it. This is one of those underrated needle-movers that can feel like an utter revelation if only you try it.

A final note about proper hydration: It may seem so simple and obvious, but you won't realize how powerful it truly is until you put it into practice. You'll be able to FEEL the benefits instantly.

Oftentimes the most simple things are the most powerful. This practice is one of them.

Phase 3: Move

Remember this: A busy man's most valuable assets are his energy and confidence. Without them, he's just a hamster running on a wheel, going nowhere fast.

Protecting your energy and confidence in the morning is like a power-up for your day.

Think of it as putting on your superhero cape before you face the world. It'll give you the boost you need to tackle the day's challenges and opportunities with ease.

Failing to do this is like playing a video game on the highest difficulty setting. Everything feels so much *harder*, you start second-guessing yourself, and you're more likely to get beat by the boss, (aka life).

Don't let that be you. Start your day off right by protecting your energy and confidence.

One of the best ways to do this is to ***get up and move.***

This is one of those things that might sound ordinary and common sensical, but when you actually DO it and experience it for yourself? It feels like an absolute revelation, setting a positive tone for the rest of the day and creating momentum that carries over into all areas of your life.

Don't get hung up on what type of movement you should do. It doesn't matter if you're doing a quick bodyweight workout at home or in your hotel room, lifting dumbbells, hitting the gym, or just going for a walk — the important thing is that you're doing *something* to move your body.

As a coach to high performers for more than ten years, I've seen firsthand how easy it is for guys with the best intentions to put off their workout or movement until later in the day. But as we all know, "later" rarely comes. Work projects pile up, the kids get sick, or your significant other needs you to do something. By the time the dust settles, you're too tired to even think about working out.

Still need convincing? Let me tell you what the science says about how this simple habit can significantly impact your energy levels and spur weight loss.

When you exercise in the morning, your body releases endorphins, which are natural mood boosters and can help to reduce stress and improve overall well-being. This can help you start your day with a positive mindset and a boost of energy that can last throughout the day.

Working out in the morning also increases your body's ability to burn fat. What's not to like about *that*?

Oh, and would you like to supercharge your results? Then do this morning movement on an empty stomach. Research has found that when you exercise in the morning on an empty stomach, your body is forced to burn stored fat for fuel instead of relying on the energy from your last meal.

So, don't hit snooze. GET UP and MOVE.

Start small by going for a simple walk or consider doing one of these quick and efficient movements here: *www.acceleratedmethod.com/movement*

In Chapter 9, I'll be uncovering the most efficient and effective movement secrets to help you maximize your results, no matter how busy your schedule is.

Phase 4: Contrast Shower

A contrast shower is when you alternate between warm and cold water throughout the duration of your shower.

I know what you're thinking — no one wants to take a cold shower!

But hear me out. I thought the same thing. Let me say a few things and you'll understand why I'm so excited about this phase of the protocol.

First of all, we're only talking about brief spurts of cold water here. No one is asking you to take an entirely cold shower.

Now, check out the science on this because this is where it gets super fascinating.

Studies have shown that once the body gets hit with any kind of cold exposure, it releases norepinephrine in the bloodstream.

What is that, and why is it important? Well, norepinephrine is a hormone and neurotransmitter that promotes alertness and helps with overall mood. Cold exposure also increases focus and energy as you warm up from the cold.

You want that in plain terms? Okay, here it is: Once you turn off the water and step out of your contrast shower, you feel FREAKING AMAZING! I'm sorry for the all-CAPS! But they're necessary because until you experience it for yourself, it's hard to adequately describe how energized you feel after a shower in which you have alternated between hot and cold water.

If you try this, you'll find that you instantly feel a tingly, energetic power — both physically and mentally — and not just for a few seconds either. It lasts for a good long while.

It's a morning boost like no other, believe me.

There are some other benefits you can expect, too. You will:

- Burn more fat
- Lower inflammation within the body
- Feel less aches and pains
- Recover from injuries faster
- Improve your overall sleep quality
- Strengthen your immune system

But my favorite benefit? It just might be the increased

mental resilience. Let's face it, being exposed to any type of cold water, especially in the morning, doesn't sound like fun.

But when you choose to embrace a bit of the cold in the morning, you program your brain to take action despite how you may feel. This can pay dividends in all areas of your life.

So, how exactly do you alternate the hot and cold water?

I suggest you ease into it. Start by taking your warm shower and then the last 10 to 20 seconds turn the water to cold.

Once you've done that for a few days, I challenge you to alternate the water from warm to cold. 20 seconds cold and 10 seconds warm until you've finished showering.

You get the idea. Find a combination that works for you.

And then enjoy the incredible boost you'll receive!

Oxygen Mask Protocol Bonus Amplifiers

I have a couple of bonus "amplifiers" I'd like to recommend for your daily routine. These are quite effective and will turbo-charge your mental and physical state.

Oxygen Mask Protocol Bonus Amplifier #1

Get Exposure to Light:

Light is the single most important element for setting your circadian clock, which is your internal 24-hour rhythm. And morning light is key to setting that in motion for the rest of your day.

The number of health benefits from exposing yourself to light in the morning are staggering. They include:

1. **Regulating your body's natural sleep-wake cycle.** Exposing yourself to light in the morning helps "reset" your internal clock, making it easier for you to fall asleep at night and wake up feeling fully rested in the morning.

2. **Improving your mood** and reducing symptoms of depression.

3. **Boosting your energy levels.**

4. **Enhancing cognitive function.** One experiment showed that office workers who got more bright morning light for five days found it easier to make decisions and scored 79 percent higher on cognitive tests. Your ability to concentrate and pay attention may be sharpened, too.

5. **Better weight control.** Studies show that morning light may affect the hormones leptin, (the hormone that makes you feel full), and ghrelin, (the hunger hormone), in ways that promote a healthy body weight. WebMD reports that researchers at Northwestern University found that people who got most of their bright light exposure before noon

weighed a little less — 1.4 pounds, on average — than those exposed to most bright light in the evening. That may not seem like a lot, but simply having your hormones operate normally is reason enough to expose yourself to light as soon as you wake up.

Bottom line, getting light in the morning can help you to feel more alert and energized, and may have a number of other positive effects on your physical and mental health.

What if it's cloudy?

While bright, direct sunlight is the most effective source of light for regulating your body's internal clock and obtaining the other potential health benefits of light exposure, it is still possible to get some benefits from light on cloudy or overcast days.

On cloudy days, you may need to spend more time in the light to get the same effects as you would on a sunny day. For example, you may need to spend 30 to 60 minutes in a brightly lit room to get the same benefits as 10 to 15 minutes of direct sunlight. Just do what you can to reap the benefits.

It is also possible to use artificial light sources, such as light therapy lamps, to help regulate your body's internal clock and improve mood. Light therapy lamps are designed to mimic the natural light spectrum, and they can be an effective way to get light exposure when it is not possible to spend time outside.

While bright sunlight is the most effective source of light for improving health and well-being, it is still possible to get some benefits from light exposure on cloudy days through the use of artificial light sources.

What if you're awake before the sun comes up?

If you are awake before the sun comes up, you may not have access to natural light to help regulate your body's internal clock and improve your mood.

In this case, you can use artificial light sources to help get the benefits of light exposure.

One option is to use a light therapy lamp, which is designed to mimic the natural light spectrum and can be used to help regulate your body's internal clock and improve mood.

In addition to using a light therapy lamp, you can also try to get as much natural light as possible during the day by opening your curtains and blinds and spending time outside when the sun is up.

Of course, it's important to remember to use sunscreen and protect your skin when spending time in the sun, especially during the middle of the day when the sun's rays are the strongest. It is also important to be mindful of the risk of skin cancer and to take steps to protect yourself from excessive sun exposure.

Oxygen Mask Protocol Bonus Amplifier #2

Jumpstart Your Morning by Adding a Quality Greens Mix

It's no secret most people don't eat enough vegetables. Greens powders are dietary supplements that make it easy for you to reach your daily recommended vegetable intake. You can mix them in water or include them in smoothies. Either way, you'll give yourself a ton of vitamins and minerals you might not get otherwise.

Here are some benefits of taking a high quality greens supplement:

- They strengthen immune function.
- They reduce inflammation in the body, (and less inflammation means less pain).
- They help with digestion.
- They improve liver function.
- They act as a detoxifier.
- They naturally improve your energy level.

Well, there you have it! The condensed version of my Oxygen Mask Protocol. I say "condensed" because I custom design more elaborate protocols for my private clients. I'm able to do this because everyone's needs are different and so I always make a point to customize everything carefully for each client.

The important thing to remember is this: Protecting your time and putting yourself first doesn't have to take long.

We're talking less than 30 minutes to show up for *you* so that you can show up for everyone else in your world at a much higher level.

Would you like to hear more about how I customize and expand this protocol for guys like yourself? I'd love to tell you more about how we add in the "AMP" supplementation stack, as well as expand on my "All Day Energy Formula" that helps clients recapture the same energy, enthusiasm, and body from their early 20s and 30s.

It starts with amplifying your mornings, and I make sure to personally tailor routines that fit within your lifestyle. The whole goal is to meet you where YOU are so that you can have the energy, focus, and mental clarity to dominate at work and be "truly present" at home.

It would be hard to overstate how amazing it is to wake up each day knowing you'll be able to power through each day without even trying — and without that two o'clock Starbucks or Red Bull boost either.

If it sounds too simple, you'd be right — it IS! It's taken me years of research, trial, and error to get it this simple, and I can tell you that every busy person loves its 1-2-3 simplicity. It's what makes it so easy to follow.

For more information on the exact formula, pick a time to chat about it here:
https://www.acceleratedmethod.com/call

Key Chapter Takeaways

The Oxygen Mask Protocol works under the assumption that even if you understand hormones, inflammation, and the concept of health debt, you will not succeed if you do not prioritize yourself first. It's not selfish; it's making sure that you can bring the best YOU to your family and bring your "A" game to your career.

The Oxygen Mask Protocol includes these very simple, but highly effective, routines:

- **The Morning Blackout.** With your devices turned off, make sure you get what you need before inviting others into your mental space.
- **Hyper Hydrate.** Rehydrate your cells first thing each morning for a day-long foundation of clarity and energy. (And yes, you can still have your coffee! Just delay it 1-2 hours for the optimal hormonal experience described in this chapter.)
- **Movement.** Start your day off right by protecting your energy and confidence by getting up and moving. It doesn't matter if you're doing a quick bodyweight or dumbbell workout from home, hitting the local or hotel gym, or just going for a walk, the important thing is that you're

moving your body and taking care of yourself.

- **Contrast Shower.** Instantly boost your energy, your mood and weight loss efforts by taking a contrast shower. Start by taking your warm shower and then the last 10 to 20 seconds turn the water to cold. Once you've done that for a few days, I challenge you to alternate the water from warm to cold. 20 seconds cold and 10 seconds warm until you've finished showering.
- **Consider adding in the bonus "amplifiers" to your morning routine** by getting exposure to natural light and taking a quality greens mix. These are quite effective and will turbo-charge your mental and physical state.

CASE STUDY

Josh H., Nevada, Business Owner and High-Performing Attorney

"The energy I have now compared to what I was before, is quite dramatic."

"The first thing I noticed within a couple of days was the energy level picked up. If I look back on myself three months ago, I would close my door at work, lay on a couch for two or three hours and do emails. I was productive, but I was just exhausted.

So in my mind I was like, "I'm working, I'm working, this is okay." And on paper it was okay, but I was just depleted, exhausted, no energy. In the first week of the program, I had energy all day long, sustainable energy that I hadn't had for years. And still to this day I maintain that. It's the energy, the mindset, the optimism, and how I look forward to the day- instead of waking up exhausted — that does not happen anymore. The mental and the emotional side of things, as well as the energy I have now compared to what I was before is quite dramatic and worth the price alone.

I have the energy to lead my team at work. Before, I don't think they were looking at me with much confidence. I didn't even realize it at the time. Now I have the energy, I have more mental clarity. I tackle projects faster, which has allowed me to really accomplish a lot more in a day, in a week, in a month then I used to, even three months ago. That's been really really big."

— Josh H., Nevada, Business Owner and High-Performing Attorney

CHAPTER 7

Snooze or Lose: The Surprising (and Alarming) Science of Sleep

I'm about to blow your mind on what you might THINK is an ordinary topic, but in reality is one of the most fundamental and crucial ways to go from sick and tired to back on fire.

That topic is ...

SLEEP!

And yeah, I totally get it ...

Most of the high-performing men I've had the pleasure of working with usually tend to see rest as more of a "luxury" than a necessity.

I get it because I used to think exactly the same thing.

Before I figured all this stuff out, most of the time when I was "working" (air quotes) what I was actually doing was simply trying to get my head in the game! Not to mention when I actually DID start to work, it wasn't long before I found myself in the quicksand of an afternoon lull, feeling like I needed a nap just to make it to the end of the day. (Remember the concept of Health Debt we discussed in Chapter 4? I was overextended on that type of debt, to say the least.)

I quickly discovered something important:

Inconsistent energy is the single biggest indicator of a lack of quality sleep.

If you're unable to get done what you need to during your workday, you'll find yourself constantly playing catch up.

Here's what that looks like: experiencing afternoon crashes, feeling like a "dead man walking" by the end of the day, feeling foggy, forgetting things, waking up in the morning feeling like a zombie ... and then trying to redeem it all during weekends, (aka "recovery days").

Whew. Does any of that sound familiar? And if so, wouldn't you rather have FUN on the weekends rather than simply lay on the couch in recovery mode? (I'm pretty sure I know how your family would answer that one.)

You CAN, you know. It all comes down to sleep.

Now, at this point you might be wondering why we're addressing the issue of sleep AFTER we've just discussed the Oxygen Mask Protocol, which begins first thing in the morning. Isn't that backwards?

Actually, no. Here's why: It's all in the timing. You see, a successful morning routine starts with a good night's rest. Just like a sturdy foundation is crucial for a tall building, adequate amounts of high-quality sleep are crucial for maintaining the energy and focus necessary to put yourself first as outlined in the Oxygen Mask Protocol.

Without consistently good sleep, trying to stick to your morning routine is nearly impossible.

Other health methods will generally tell you that the foundation for obtaining great energy, feeling better, and losing that extra weight starts with diet and exercise. And though those *do* play a critical role, no question.

But make no mistake: Getting quality sleep is the single biggest foundational principle when it comes to feeling and looking better and having more energy.

Deep, restful sleep is our best opportunity to restore, recharge and reboot our entire operating system. When we rob ourselves of sleep, we're making it next to impossible to function and produce at a high level.

In fact, studies have proven that going on six hours or less of sleep consistently can reduce our functioning to the level of someone who is legally drunk. That might sound crazy, but they have a way of measuring these things as it relates to memory and decision making. So believe it.

Without sufficient sleep, our ability to process, recall, and retain new information suffers greatly. Those are obviously crucial areas to maintain if you want to continue advancing in your career.

Not only that, but other research has proven that

chronically bad sleep screws up our hormones, contributes to weight gain, ages us faster, makes us prone to becoming sick more often, and drains our overall focus and productivity.

The good news: Adequate sleep can quickly fix all this.

We high performers need quality sleep for three main reasons:

1. **Emotional regulation:** Lack of quality sleep can lead to emotional instability and overreactions in daily life, both at home and at work. Studies have shown that sleep deprivation can wreak the same havoc on your emotions as if you were under the influence of alcohol.

2. **Cognitive function:** Adequate sleep is crucial for the brain's ability to process and consolidate information. During sleep, the brain organizes and stores important information in long-term memory, discarding unnecessary information. Studies show that even a moderate amount of sleep deprivation can significantly reduce the ability to learn, store, and recall information. Needless to say, this could hurt your earning potential and make getting ahead that much tougher.

3. **Weight control:** Poor sleep disrupts the balance of hormones that regulate hunger and appetite. When you're sleep-deprived, your body produces higher levels of the hormone ghrelin, known as the "hunger hormone." It also suppresses leptin, the hormone that sends you the signal that you're

full. This leads to cravings for high-calorie, sugary foods. But wait, there's more: A lack of sleep also increases cortisol, which leads to more belly fat and extra pounds overall. It messes with your glucose and insulin metabolism, which is a greased chute to obesity and type 2 diabetes. And, to top it all off, when you're tired, you're less motivated to exercise and engage in all the activities that promote good health.

Let me summarize all the reasons you should prioritize sleep, like, yesterday:

- It helps regulate our mood. (Think how young kids act when they don't get enough sleep ... 'nuff said!)
- It keeps us sharp and firing on all cylinders, maintaining mental clarity at an all-time high while destroying brain fog.
- Helps regulate our metabolism, including blood sugar and insulin levels, which can prevent obesity, belly fat, and type 2 diabetes.
- Helps lower inflammation.
- Increases your zest for life and keeps your motivation high which means you'll enthusiastically begin doing all the things that are good for you.

So hopefully, you're getting the point that sleep is not just important, but essential. And look, I fully realize I may not be the first one to tell you about this. Thankfully, sleep is a health topic that has attracted some much-needed attention lately. However, there's a lot of information out there, and I want to simplify this for you because I know you're busy.

Before I tell you exactly how to fix your sleep so that you can bounce out of bed and power through your day like never before, let me share a quick story.

Steven's Story

My client Steven is a business leader in the government sector. He's a high performer with an impressive track record of success.

Like many of us, Steven lived by a motto that dismissed sleep as little more than an unimportant obstacle on the road to success.

Here's something he used to say all the time:

"I'll sleep when I'm dead."

Sound familiar?

If you're not saying that exact thing, then maybe you're saying (or thinking) one of the following:

"Well, I'm a guy that doesn't need a lot of sleep."

"I can power through when I need to."

"I'll be fine — it's just a state of mind."

No, no, no! Hopefully by the time you finish this chapter, you'll see how misguided — dangerous, even — those rationalizations are.

Anyway, before I started working with Steven, a typical weekday saw him getting very little sleep — often just 2-3 hours and perhaps four to five hours at best.

He figured he could catch up on weekends. This is known as trying to "bank" sleep, but unfortunately, this is a doomed strategy that has its limits. Even worse, he missed out on crucial family time because he would be sleeping most of the weekend.

Here's how his week would unfold:

Mondays weren't too bad.

By Tuesday, he noticed his stamina would start to dip.

By Wednesday, he needed an extra coffee or two just to stay alert.

By Thursday, his caffeine intake started to rise to dangerously high levels.

And come Friday? On Fridays, he was ready for someone to put him out of his misery! *That's* how utterly exhausted he felt.

Because so many of us dismiss the importance of sleep, it's often a "hidden" problem. In Steven's case, I was able to show him that sleep was one of the missing pieces holding him back from the success and happiness he was missing out on.

And so we developed a plan to end this unhealthy, unsustainable pattern. A plan that worked for HIM.

He now knows, beyond the shadow of a doubt, how crucial it is to get a good night's rest.

Why am I sharing this with you?

Because he's not the only one devaluing sleep — our entire culture is guilty of it.

In fact, the average American only gets a measly six and a half hours of sleep each night … at best.

I'll be honest, I used to be one of those guys who thought that by banking my sleep on weekends, I could power through the week with plenty of all-day energy.

It sounds logical, right?

Well, here's the thing:

Sleep doesn't work the same way as socking away money in a financial institution.

If you want to burst with energy all week long, you've got to treat your body right by getting plenty of slumber.

That means getting at least seven hours of quality sleep each night, going to bed at the same time, *and* waking up at the same time.

If you do this, you'll find yourself grabbing fewer cups of coffee and fewer sugary foods and firing on all cylinders both physically and mentally.

Now, if you think you're getting enough sleep, but you still find yourself dragging ass at 3 in the afternoon

where you feel like you need a nap underneath your desk just to push through the day, this may be why...

Here let me phrase this in the form of a question:

Do you ever come home after a long day of work and suddenly, (almost inexplicably), find yourself on the couch?

And I don't just mean "sitting on" the couch — I mean, you are *buried* halfway between the creases, almost as if the couch is trying to swallow you whole.

Pretty soon you're scrolling on your phone, catching up on bad news, watching SportsCenter, or binge-watching that new Netflix or HBO show ... and before you know it, it's almost midnight.

If this sounds familiar, don't feel bad. It's not just you.

I had a conversation the other day with a gentleman who was in this exact situation.

"Funny thing is," he told me, "doing this didn't help me feel more rested. It just made me more tired."

Actually, that makes perfect sense.

This is because his overall sleep quality wasn't where it needed to be. Not only was he tired and out of it, he felt like absolute *shit*.

After talking to dozens of guys in this same boat, here's what I've learned. (Cue drum roll...)

Staying up past 11 p.m., looking at screens, will seriously mess with your quality of sleep.

Which will then seriously mess with your quality of life.

It doesn't matter whether you're "relaxing" in front of the TV or doing more work on your computer, the effect is the same.

Look, this is not my own bias talking. There's plenty of serious evidence to back it up.

Here's some basic science that will explain what's going on with your messed-up sleep patterns:

There's a small mass of cells in your brain known as the "habenula," and this part of the brain plays a big role in your circadian rhythm.

Here's what happens: When you stay up past 11 p.m. binge-watching on HBO, (or whatever your streaming platform of choice is), you're manually overriding your brain's reminders that it's time to sleep.

Now, your brain has no idea it's some ungodly hour of the night (or morning).

On top of that, your habenula kicks into gear and becomes active.

And by "active," I mean it actually suppresses your dopamine levels.

Dopamine is a neurotransmitter that is associated with feelings of pleasure and reward.

And when you make a habit out of suppressing your dopamine levels every night, it can actually cause mild to severe depression.

That's right, staying up late staring at screens literally makes you depressed.

I can guess what you're thinking right now:

"Okay, Logan, but is it really that big of a deal, though, if I just knock out one more project?"

"Let me just check one more email ... and THEN I'll turn in. No big deal."

"It's just one more episode ... how could that hurt?

Trust me, it CAN hurt. And it's so easy to rationalize as to become a danger to your health.

The next time you're tempted to do "just one more" thing using your screen, remember that you are shutting off the valve to your dopamine supply, which will in all likelihood lead you to feeling like total shit.

And what happens when you feel like total shit?

You start looking for ways to feel more comfortable and less shitty.

That might mean raiding the pantry for your kids' snacks. Or reaching for a cocktail from the back of the fridge.

Whatever it is that you do to comfort yourself after a long hard day at work — resulting in you staying up late — I got you.

Biologically speaking, that's not who you *really* are. It's definitely not who you want to be.

But if you've ever found yourself in this situation, or if this is your current *modus operandi*, I want to encourage you to be more mindful so you can catch yourself and start changing this habit *now.*

Start during the workweek, (when you know you need to be at the top of your game), to get to bed as soon as reasonably possible.

Ideally, before 11 p.m.

If it sounds unreasonable to be asleep by 11, at least try going to bed by 11:30.

Do whatever you have to do to take that first step.

When the weekend comes and you want to let your hair down a little bit, go ahead and stay up late if you want. I'm not saying your head has to hit the pillow by 9:45 every night for the rest of your life, (and if I did, I'd be a total hypocrite myself).

Just remember, though, there's a reason that kids have bedtimes.

We may be adults who can make our own decisions, but we still need that precious time to recharge.

And that's why, at the risk of coming off like the parent tapping his watch to tell you it's time to go to bed, I need to say the following:

You will feel a lot better and experience a much

higher quality of life if you start going to bed slightly before 11 p.m.

Now, obviously you're an adult, and you know yourself and your own life situation best.

But the current science, (not to mention my own experience and that of my clients), agrees that once you start going to bed at a reasonable time, you'll notice other amazing things start to happen in your life, too.

You'll be able to focus better at your work meetings and be able to tackle whatever's on your agenda with confidence.

You'll be able to carry that energy with you home to your loved ones and be able to support them with whatever they're going through.

You'll start shedding excess weight and feel way better about the guy in the mirror looking back at you.

All that being said, if you want to unleash endless energy, mental clarity, and fire on all cylinders, — both physically and mentally ALL of the time — then understand that it's critical for you to get to bed before 11 p.m. And then get at least seven hours of quality sleep, going to bed at the same time each night, and then repeating this as consistently as you can most nights of the week.

There's no more straightforward way to say it than that, but it still doesn't make it easy.

When I speak to men struggling with their health and depleted energy levels, I'll ask them how much sleep they are getting a night, and usually, they are embarrassed to tell me.

As I mentioned, It's recommended to get 7-8 hours of (quality) sleep a night. However, most men I work with are getting 5 or 6 hours, and it's disrupted sleep.

Now, notice I said 7-8 hours of *quality* sleep.

Let me tell you why that's so crucial.

Deep Sleep for Deep Success: Why Sleep Is a Game of Quality, Not Just Quantity

When it comes to sleep, it's not all about the quantity- it's about the quality!

You can sleep for hours, but if the quality of your sleep is poor, you're still going to wake up feeling groggy and unrested. But when you get high-quality sleep, it's like hitting a reset button on your entire body and mind.

Seriously, this works so well it can feel like magic. Have you ever been on a much-needed vacation, and you wake up that first morning so deeply rested that you feel like a brand new person?

You don't have to be on vacation to achieve that! Let me explain how.

When it comes to sleep, there's a lot more going on than just closing your eyes and snoring. Your body goes through different stages of sleep, each one serving a specific purpose.

First, there's light sleep, where your body is in a drowsy state, and your brain is producing alpha and theta waves. This is where you're in that half-awake, half-asleep state.

Then, you move into the transition stage of sleep, where your body temperature drops, your heart rate slows down, and your brain starts producing what's known as sleep spindles and K-complexes. This is where you're in a deeper slumber, and it's harder to wake you up.

Next, there's the deep sleep stage, also known as the "beauty sleep" stage. This is when your brain is producing mostly delta waves, and your body is doing some serious repair work — rebuilding tissues, muscles, and bones. It's like your body's own personal construction site.

And finally, there's the REM (Rapid Eye Movement) stage, where your brain is active and produces similar brain waves as when you're awake. This is when you're dreaming, and it's also when your brain is consolidating memories and information.

Now, to truly get quality sleep, your body needs to go through all of these stages in the right sequence. And in order to function optimally the next day, your aim should be to complete around five sleep cycles per night, (which equals out to seven to eight hours a night).

Imagine if your body skips the deep sleep stage — it would be like your construction site shutting down before it could finish its work. Your body wouldn't be able to repair itself.

Or, let's say your body spends too much time in the light

sleep stage — it would be like your brain was stuck in a loop, not getting the rest it needed. And that's why quality sleep is so important: It's like all the puzzle pieces coming together.

So, to sum it up, quality sleep is like a symphony where all the stages of sleep are played in the right order and for the right duration. It's when your body and brain get the chance to repair, restore, and rejuvenate themselves. And when this happens consistently, you'll wake up feeling truly rested, "on fire," and ready to take on the world.

Now, at this point, you're probably thinking to yourself, "Wow, this all sounds great, but how am I going to make it happen?"

Don't worry, I got you.

Let's turn those sweet dreams into a reality and make better sleep a top priority, shall we?

The secret to a good night's sleep is that it starts much earlier than bedtime. If you are racing around all day and then collapsing into bed without any transition period at all, then you're going to get lousy sleep.

One of the keys to high-quality sleep is to structure your day so that you are ready to rest by the time you get to bedtime. This is such an effective and underrated tip that I developed a specific pre-bedtime routine around this truth.

I call it **The 1-3-2-1 Protocol**. This is something I developed to help promote a healthy night's sleep so that you can wake up feeling rested and ready to hit the ground running.

Here's How The 1-3-2-1 Protocol Works:

1-3-2-1

1 p.m. Stop consuming all caffeine or other stimulants.

Why? Well, caffeine works by blocking the action of a neurotransmitter called adenosine in the brain. Adenosine is a chemical that builds up over the course of the day and contributes to feelings of sleepiness. When caffeine blocks adenosine, it can lead to increased alertness and energy.

So why stop at 1 o'clock? It's because caffeine has a half-life of around 5-6 hours, which means that 50 percent of the caffeine you had in the afternoon is still circulating in your body as you near bedtime.

To extend the math even further, that means 25 percent of that caffeine is still blocking the sleepiness chemical in your brain 10 hours later! That's a significant obstacle to falling asleep. It leads to poor sleep quality for obvious reasons.

1-**3**-2-1

3 hours before bed, have your last BIG meal of the day. (Dinner, for most of us.)

If you're serious about getting some quality shut-eye, it's time to pay attention to the clock... and your stomach. You see, when we eat a big heavy meal close to bedtime, our body has to work overtime to digest it. This can lead to indigestion, discomfort, and even heartburn. So, here's the deal: Aim to finish your last big meal of the day at least three hours before bedtime. Can you still have a light snack after your last big meal? Sure, it won't kill ya. Just make sure to give it two hours to digest before hitting the hay. Trust me, your stomach (and your sleep) will thank you.

Oh, and there's one more critical component to the "3 hours before bedtime" rule, and this is important.

Brace yourself because here it is: Booze.

Sure, that nightcap may take the edge off at first, but it's actually doing more harm than good when it comes to your sleep.

Think of it like this:

Imagine your sleep as a badass action movie star who needs to be ready for his next scene every night.

Each night, you give it the proper training and preparation, allowing it to perform at its very best the next day.

But when you introduce alcohol into the mix, it's like introducing a stunt double in the middle of the film. He might kinda LOOK like you... and he might be a half-decent stand-in for you *temporarily*... but he's not you at your best, not even close! He doesn't know your lines and he's nothing more than a shadow of your full potential.

When you crack open a cold one shortly before bed, alcohol will disrupt your natural sleep cycle, causing more shallow and fragmented sleep. You simply won't get that deep, restful sleep your body craves. Not only does this affect the quality of sleep, but it also impacts the quantity of sleep. This is particularly harmful because it interferes with the REM sleep stage, which is essential for cognitive and emotional well-being.

So, if you want to wake up feeling like a badass action movie star — the real one, not some lame stand-in — then cut off alcohol at least three hours before bedtime.

1-3-**2**-1

2 Hours Before Bed, shut off ALL work and conduct a brain dump to get everything out of your head on paper to prepare for the next day.

You know that feeling when you're lying in bed, trying to fall asleep, but your mind just won't shut off? It's the bane of our existence, but I've got a solution for you. It's called a work shutdown routine, and it's a total game-changer.

This is a two-step process.

The first step is: No work two hours before bed. And I mean *none*. Seriously. That means no more emails, no more phone calls, no more meetings, no more work-related items, nothing whatsoever. This is necessary to allow the brain to shutdown, dissociate, and take a break from all of that.

This also includes mindlessly scrolling certain social networks. (And by "certain" I mean all the fun and popular ones. Sorry!)

The goal is to not spike your dopamine at this hour or do anything that's going to excite and stimulate your senses.

The second step: Take a little time to "brain dump" all the thoughts and to-dos that are swirling around in your head. You can do this in a notebook, on a legal pad, or on a simple sheet of paper. Doesn't matter which one. No one else is going to see this but you. It's simply you writing out whatever is on your mind that's work or task-related or whatever is on your mind, period. Just get it all out.

This will allow you to release all those thoughts so that they're not racing through your mind as you try to fall asleep.

And remember, the key is to do this at least two hours before bed. This is so that your mind has enough time to unwind and relax. It's a simple but powerful way to give your mind the break it needs to be able to recharge and be ready for the next day.

1-3-2-1

1 Hour Before Bed, aim to turn off all electronic screens and limit any exposure to blue light.

Why? Well, first let's talk about where blue light comes from. Many electronic devices, such as smartphones, tablets, laptops, and LED light bulbs, emit a significant amount of what's known as blue light. Also known as high-energy visible (HEV) light, blue has a wavelength that is similar to the light that the sun gives off during the day. It's been found to suppress the production of melatonin, which is a hormone that helps regulate your sleep-wake cycle.

Several studies show that exposure to blue light in the evening can lead to poor sleep and feeling fatigued the next day. One such study, published in the journal *Sleep Health*, found that people who were exposed to blue light for just one hour before bedtime had a harder time falling asleep, as well as a suppressed melatonin secretion by about 22 percent.

So, if you're someone who likes to watch TV or scroll through your phone before bed, it's best to limit those activities outside of the hour before bed and consider it a good idea to invest in some blue light-blocking glasses or apps that can filter out the blue light on your devices.

Aside from blocking blue light, you should aim to relax by activating your parasympathetic nervous system.

The parasympathetic nervous system is like the "relax and recharge" button for your body. Think of the parasympathetic nervous system as the "yoga master" of your body, helping you to relax and find inner peace.

When your body is in a state of rest and digestion, the parasympathetic nervous system is active. It slows down your heart rate, increases blood flow to your digestive tract, and makes it easier for you to relax and rest. It's like a dimmer switch for your body's energy levels, helping you to wind down and recharge after a long day.

You can activate your parasympathetic nervous system even further by reading a non-stimulating book before bed, taking a warm shower (or bath), or practicing deep breathing exercises.

If you still find it difficult to quiet your mind and get into a relaxed state to sleep, below are a couple of sleep supplements to consider.

Two Sleep Supplements to Help You Dream Big and Sleep Deeply

#1- Magnesium

Yes, I know you've heard of magnesium. And I know it's not the most exciting supplement out there, but trust me, it's a very underrated secret weapon for getting a good night's sleep.

Here's the deal: Magnesium helps regulate your body's levels of melatonin, a hormone that plays a big role in regulating your sleep-wake cycle.

By taking magnesium before bed, you're giving your body a little extra boost to help you fall asleep faster and stay asleep longer.

#2- Ashwagandha

In an earlier chapter, I mentioned Ashwagandha as one

of my top recommended supplements to clients. One of the primary reasons is just how effective it is at putting you in a relaxed state. This powerful herb has a wide range of benefits, but it's particularly effective when it comes to helping people relax and get a good night's sleep.

Ashwagandha is an adaptogen, meaning it helps the body cope with stress. It is also known to help improve sleep quality and reduce insomnia. It is a powerful supplement to take before bed because it can help reduce the racing thoughts and anxiety that often keep people awake at night.

Here's a fun way to think about it:

Imagine Ashwagandha as a personal bodyguard for your mind. It's like having a bouncer at the door of your brain, keeping out all the negative thoughts and worries that want to keep you awake.

Here's a short list of what it does:

- It fights off all the cortisol, (the hormone that makes you feel like you're about to jump out of your skin), in your body.
- It increases the levels of GABA, (an amino acid that acts as an inhibitory neurotransmitter in the brain, helping reduce anxiety and promote relaxation).
- It boosts your levels of serotonin, (sometimes known as "the happy chemical"), which will help you feel calm and relaxed.

Bottom line: with Ashwagandha on the job, you can finally get the peaceful night's sleep you deserve.

Of course, before trying either of these supplements for a better night's sleep, (or any supplements at all), it's always important to check with a doctor. Your physician knows your body and health history better than anyone else and can help ensure that any supplements you're considering are safe and appropriate for you. This is especially important if you're currently taking any medications or have any underlying health conditions.

Let's Put This Issue to Bed (see what I did there?)

I've done my best to get your attention on this issue of sleep. That's because it's a total game-changer for anyone who embraces it. But I also know it can be hard to take that first step.

Maybe you have questions, or you're wondering "will this really make a difference for me?"

Maybe you could just use some extra support getting started.

That's what I'm here for.

You see, there is so much more I cover on the importance of sleep with my clients, including a system that helps calculate the precise time someone should go to sleep to wake up feeling refreshed based on their specific lifestyle factors, as well as additional sleep supplementation for those who really have a tough time falling — and staying

— asleep. All of this is shared in a more customizable approach when working directly with my clients as I know everybody has a unique lifestyle and household situation. (And hopefully, at the very least, you're starting to see the value in prioritizing it highly.)

If you want a shortcut to this whole process, then schedule a call to see how I can radically shorten the time it takes to implement everything we've talked about so far.

You don't have to do this alone. I have a systematic way to deliver the results you want without all the trial and error.

The link below will take you to a page where you can schedule a friendly, no-pressure chat with me or my team that explains how I can help you get the results you want and need.

https://www.acceleratedmethod.com/call

Key Chapter Takeaways

- Sleep is an absolute necessity, not a luxury.
- Inconsistent energy is the single biggest indicator of a lack of quality sleep.
- The list of things that sleep can remedy or create is astounding: It can help fix your hormones, become your biggest

ally in losing weight, will help you look younger, prevent you from getting sick as often, and ramp up your overall focus and productivity.

- Staying up past 11 p.m. will seriously mess with your quality of sleep more than you would ever guess.
- Use the 1-3-2-1 Protocol as a pre-bedtime routine to give yourself the best chance of a quality night of deep, restorative sleep.
- Consider taking magnesium and Ashwagandha as two supplements to help you with your sleep.

CASE STUDY

Steven P., Washington, D.C., High-Performing Business Leader

"I look more like I looked five, six, 10 years ago. Across the board, it works, and it's been awesome."

"I was to the point where I was tired of being tired. Tired of where my energy was at, where I was feeling physically, where I was at with sleep. I was bored trying to figure it out myself, and I wasn't liking my results with my team. And wanted to try something different and kind of attack the problem holistically. My energy was drained and felt like on the weekends I had to stock back up. Since entering the program, my energy and confidence were up up up in the span of the first couple weeks. And they've stayed up. Physically, it's crazy. I'm down 27 pounds. Other measurements, especially around the gut, were five to six inches slimmer. My pants don't fit well anymore, they're too loose. We're getting to where they are going to have to be replaced or tailored. I look more like I looked five, six, 10 years ago. Across the board, it works, and it's been awesome."

— Steven P., Washington, D.C., High-Performing Business Leader

CHAPTER 8

Eat to Win: Unlocking the Power of Proper Nutrition for Maximum Performance

Have you ever stopped to think about how you're fueling your body?

We all know the importance of maintaining our cars for optimal performance, but when it comes to our own bodies, we often neglect the importance of proper nutrition.

You see, just like a high-performance sports car, our bodies need the right kind of fuel to run at their best. But instead of filling up with premium gasoline, the majority of guys I see are pouring into their gas tanks the equivalent of cheap, greasy fast food for breakfast, lunch, and dinner. And instead of a proper tune-up, they're relying on caffeine to get them through the day and alcohol to take the edge off at night.

Oof. That's a recipe for a mechanical breakdown. And it's no wonder they feel sluggish and have gained an unwanted spare tire around the middle. (It's my last automotive metaphor, I promise!)

So much of this comes down to one simple reason:

They're simply not giving their body the proper nutrition it needs to function at its peak.

And trust me, I get it.

When you're busy juggling all those balls in the air, it's too easy to pull up to a drive-through window and shout your order into a loudspeaker, (and then decide if you want fries with that).

Ditto for a few beers or cocktails on the couch at night. But here's the thing: How we treat and fuel our bodies on a daily basis has a huge impact on how we feel, look, and perform.

I know you know this already. But it's even more important than you think.

The adage, "garbage in, garbage out," has never been truer when it comes to our health. But what does that actually mean?

Well, let's break it down.

To obtain sustained energy and also boost your weight loss efforts, we must focus on three main factors:

1. Regulating our blood sugars
2. Stabilizing our insulin response
3. Mitigating inflammation in our body

Think of it like this: Our blood sugar is like a car's RPM gauge on the dashboard. If it's too low, we're running (and *feeling*) sluggish. But if it's too high, we're in danger of crashing. By regulating our blood sugar, we can ensure we have smooth, sustained energy throughout the entire day.

(That's right, I'm back with the automotive metaphors...)

Next, our insulin response is like a carburetor. If it's not working properly, your vehicle can't efficiently process the fuel, (meaning you get fatigued more easily and you get hangry all the time). By stabilizing our insulin response, we can ensure our body is using the fuel in the most efficient way possible, which helps with weight loss.

Finally, inflammation in our body is like a car's check engine light. It's a bright red signal that tells us something's not working properly. By mitigating inflammation in our body, we can ensure our body is running smoothly.

Now that you understand a little more about how things operate underneath the hood, so to speak, it's time to give you the tools and tips to turbocharge your engine so you can fuel up with the premium gasoline your body needs for optimal performance and shedding those extra pounds.

Let's begin with the first step of our plan:

Step #1 - Replace sugar and gluten with nutrient-dense choices like high quality protein, healthy fats, and fibrous vegetables

Eating a diet high in sugar and gluten can lead to a rollercoaster of energy levels throughout the day. This is why that mid-morning donut or bagel gives you that late morning sugar rush, only to leave you feeling tired and sluggish a little while later. These foods spike your blood sugar, causing a quick burst of energy, followed by an inevitable crash.

On the other hand, when you eat high-quality protein, healthy fats, and fibrous foods like vegetables, you enjoy sustained energy throughout the day. Protein and healthy fats take longer for the body to digest, which means they provide a steady source of energy. (That's also why a big glass of orange juice spikes your blood sugar in a proverbial, if not literal, heartbeat.)

Vegetables, especially non-starchy ones, are low in calories but high in fiber and other essential nutrients that support overall health. And yes, I realize that vegetables are about the unsexiest food I can mention here, but it's easy to get creative with them, too. For example, dipping carrot sticks or celery stalks into some hummus makes for a healthy snack that's also really tasty.

And look, if you need more motivation in making these dietary changes, consider this: Swapping out things like cereal, bread, and orange juice for vegetables, eggs, meat sticks, and nuts will help reduce your middle aged paunch. This is because when you eat something high in sugar and gluten, your body stores excess energy as fat, particularly in the abdominal area. But when you eat a diet high in protein and healthy fats, your body burns fat for energy instead of storing it.

So if you want to avoid those awful sugar crashes and walk into conference rooms feeling like a star quarterback who "owns the room" with boundless energy, then make these simple dietary switches. You'll feel a huge difference very quickly.

It never fails to make my day when I hear one of my clients report how much more energetic they feel when they make these simple nutritional switches! And it's never surprising, either. This is one of those things that always works. Does it take a little bit of effort to make this nutritional change? I won't lie, yes it does. But once you do, you'll never look back, I promise. You'll literally change your taste buds over time and begin to actually seek out the healthier stuff (and turn down the junk without any effort whatsoever).

Keep reading to see a list of exactly what to eat to make this crucial switch.

One more thing, and this is important ...

When it comes to weight loss, it's not just about the types of foods you eat, but also your overall calorie intake. This means that eating a more balanced diet doesn't give you full license to pig out as much as you want. However, the good news is that when you eat nutrient-dense foods, you'll feel full more quickly anyway. If you eat a moderate amount of the right foods, and then wait at least 20 minutes, you will be satiated and won't think about it. (Ever wonder why it's so easy to eat three or four bowls of cereal and you feel like you could keep going? It's because you're just shoveling down low-nutrient foods that aren't giving you what your body truly needs.)

What to Start with Right Now:

1. **Identify the sources of sugar and gluten in your diet.** These foods are notorious for causing energy crashes and leaving you feeling tired and sluggish. Common sources of sugar include processed foods, sweetened beverages, and desserts. Common sources of gluten include bread, pasta, and baked goods.

   Also start reading nutrition labels. Why? Because sugar is "hiding in plain sight" in many items you might consider "healthy!" For example, many yogurts and protein bars are loaded with sugar.

   Beware of ingredients like these:

   - Corn sweetener
   - Ethyl maltol
   - Corn syrup
   - Dextrose
   - Fructose
   - Fruit juice concentrates

- Glucose
- High-fructose corn syrup

If you're eating items with any of those ingredients, take note of them and move onto the next step:

2. **Replace all processed, sugary, and energy-sapping foods** with nutrient-dense alternatives that will keep you fueled throughout the day. For example, you can replace sugary snacks with a serving of fruit, a handful of nuts, or a piece of lean protein, like chicken or fish. Replace gluten-containing foods with gluten-free alternatives such as quinoa or gluten-free bread or pasta.

3. **Incorporate more fibrous vegetables** like broccoli, cucumbers, cauliflower, spinach, and peppers into your meals. These vegetables are low in calories but high in fiber and other essential nutrients that support overall health and provide sustained energy. And don't forget, you can get creative in making vegetables more appealing. For example, as I said earlier, dipping carrot sticks or celery stalks into some hummus makes for a healthy snack that's also super tasty.

4. **Eat 2-3 high protein, healthy fat, fibrous veggie-based meals a day**. Examples of healthy fats include: olive oil, nut and seed butters, fatty fish, eggs, avocados.

Here's why the above steps are so crucial:

First, when you eat a diet high in protein, your body has to work harder to digest it, which means it takes longer to break down and that means a steadier and longer-lasting source of energy throughout the day. That means no more mid-afternoon slumps or sugar crashes!

Second, healthy fats, (like those found in avocados, nuts, and olive oil), take even longer to digest than protein, so they keep you feeling full and satisfied for longer. This can help you avoid mindless snacking and overeating, which is a common culprit in weight gain.

Third, fibrous vegetables are low in calories but high in fiber, which means they bulk up your meals without adding a lot of extra calories. Plus, they're packed with essential vitamins and minerals that your body needs to function at its best.

In short, by eating 2-3 high protein, healthy fat, fibrous veggie meals within a day, you'll avoid the ups and downs of a sugar-heavy diet, you'll be less likely to snack on empty calorie foods, you'll feel full and satisfied, and you'll be providing your body with the nutrients it needs to function at its best. It's completely win-win across the board.

Here's a quick 2-3 high protein, healthy fat, fibrous veggie meal framework you can consider following:

- **At home:** A protein-packed breakfast bowl is an example of an at-home meal that not only checks all the nutritional boxes but tastes fantastic: To prepare one, you take diced cooked bacon or sausage, scrambled eggs, sautéed spinach, diced avocado and cherry tomatoes, and then mix them all together. This meal is high in protein, healthy fats and has a fibrous veggie source. Another example is a spinach and feta cheese omelet, topped with diced avocado and a side of bacon. Both of those choices refute any notion that eating healthy can't be absolutely delicious!

- **On-the-go:** A healthy protein shake is a high-protein, low-carb snack you can take on the go. All you need is a scoop of whey protein powder, almond milk, and some frozen berries. Throw it all into a blender, pour into a Thermos, and you're good to go. A hard-boiled egg also makes for a great snack, as well as Greek yogurt, or a protein bar. (However, be sure and read the label first on any packaged bar — or any packaged product, period — to make sure it's not loaded with sugar!) Finally, meat sticks, like the ones from Chomps, are terrific, as are a handful of nuts. (Be careful with the nuts, though — those high-fat calories add up quickly. Anything more than a handful and you're asking for trouble.)

- **When at a restaurant:** Look for menu items that include lean protein and fibrous vegetables. Examples include grilled chicken or fish with a side of vegetables, salad with lean protein and a vinaigrette dressing made with olive oil and lemon juice, or a protein bowl with quinoa or brown rice, lean protein, and a variety of vegetables. Avoid items that are fried and opt for grilled or steamed options instead.

Now, let's be real, getting in your daily dose of veggies can be a bit of a drag, but don't sweat it! I've got you covered.

If you're struggling to incorporate fibrous veggies into your meals, try a power salad. A power salad is loaded with nutrient-dense ingredients like lean protein, healthy fats, and fibrous veggies, all in one convenient and delicious package. Plus, you'll be fueling your body with all the good stuff it needs to perform at its best. Just be careful with the dressing, as a power salad can quickly turn into a calorie bomb if you're not mindful of what you're pouring on top. So don't be afraid to opt for a lighter dressing or make your own with olive oil and lemon juice. When ordering out, order dressing on the side.

Check out these delicious power salads that can easily be made at home or ordered at a restaurant:

- A Caesar salad with grilled chicken breast, topped with sliced avocado, cherry tomatoes, and crumbled feta cheese. This salad is high in protein and healthy fats, and it has a good source of fibrous veggies.
- A Cobb salad with grilled chicken, hard-boiled eggs, bacon, avocado, cherry tomatoes, and blue cheese. This salad is also high in protein, healthy fats, and fibrous veggies.

- A Greek salad with grilled chicken breast, feta cheese, cherry tomatoes, cucumber, red onion, bell peppers, and Kalamata olives, topped with a vinaigrette dressing made with olive oil and lemon juice.

When ordering at a restaurant, you can ask for grilled chicken, fish or shrimp to be added to your salad. You can also ask for a vinaigrette dressing made with olive oil and lemon juice.

It's important to note that a power salad can be customized to your taste and dietary restrictions. You can add or remove ingredients as you wish, and you can use different types of protein such as grilled shrimp or tofu. You can also add some nuts or seeds, legumes such as chickpeas or lentils, to boost the protein and healthy fats content.

I'm telling you, when you learn how to mix in healthy fats and lean protein with your salads, it's a real game-changer. They are some of the most satisfying meals you'll ever have.

Now, I can hear some of you asking, "Will I ever be able to enjoy carbs again?"

The answer is a resounding "YES." You can definitely still enjoy carbs. It's all about being strategic with the types, amounts, and when you consume them. And now, as we move into the next step of fine-tuning your body to look, feel, and perform at its best, let me share a smart carb strategy that will show you how to balance carbs and stay on track. This will give you consistent energy throughout the day and allow you to shed unwanted weight from problem areas.

Step #2- Be Strategic About Your Carb Intake and Timing

Let's get one thing straight: Carbohydrates are not evil. They're simply a source of energy for the body.

However, the type, quantity, and timing of *when* to consume them can make a profound difference in your energy levels and your efforts to maintain an ideal weight.

First, let's talk about the type of carbs to consume that will deliver smooth, consistent energy rather than strapping you into a blood sugar rollercoaster.

'Smart' Carbs

Smart carbs are typically found in whole grains, vegetables, certain fruits, and legumes.

Why are they called "smart?" It's because they're known as "complex carbohydrates," which just means they *digest more slowly* than "simple carbohydrates." This prevents the spiking of insulin and helps regulate blood sugar levels. They provide a more even and sustained source of energy.

That said, not all smart carbs are created equal. For instance, some contain more gluten than others, (the lower the better).

Here's a short list of some really good smart carbohydrates to choose from:

- Sweet potatoes
- Yams
- Squash
- Pumpkin
- Potatoes (with the skin on)
- Whole grains such as quinoa and millet
- Legumes such as lentils and black beans
- Whole fruits such as avocados (yes, they are considered a fruit), berries (black, blue, and raspberry are typically the best), pears, apples, and oranges
- Non-starchy vegetables such as leafy greens, broccoli, cauliflower, cabbage, asparagus, green beans, zucchini, brussels sprouts and cucumbers
- Root vegetables such as turnips, parsnips, and carrots

Not-So-Smart Carbs

Some types of carbohydrates are more quickly absorbed and rank higher on the glycemic index (GI). This means they can spike insulin levels and cause inflammation within the body. They also tend to be higher in gluten, no surprise.

These "not-so-smart" carbs include:

- Refined grains such as white bread, pasta, and pastries
- High-fructose corn syrup and other added sugars
- Processed foods such as crackers, snack bars, and sweetened breakfast cereals
- Sugary drinks such as soda and fruit juice

Here's an interesting way to look at these two types of carbohydrates:

Think of carbohydrates like a bank account. Smart carbs, (such as certain whole grains, fruits, and vegetables), perform like steady, reliable investments that provide sustained energy and essential nutrients consistently over time. But simple carbs, (like sugar and white flour), act like risky, high-interest loans that provide a quick burst of energy but ultimately lead to "debt" in the form of sluggish afternoons and expanded waistlines.

What to Start with Right Now:

Stop eating, or at least drastically cut back, these not-so-smart carbs:

- White bread, pastries, pasta, desserts
- Anything with high-fructose corn syrup and other added sugars
- All processed foods such as crackers, snack bars, and sweetened breakfast cereals. Basically,

anything packaged in a box that can still be eaten six months or more after you purchase it, should be avoided.

- All sugary drinks such as soda and fruit juice. This includes Gatorade, Powerade, and any post-workout drink loaded with sugar. Learn to read labels!

Now let's talk about the quantity and timing of your smart carbs.

Quantity & Timing

There's a lot of biological science that explains exactly how carbs are processed in your body. I could write an entire chapter about this, but let me instead just repeat something I said earlier.

This is so important that it bears repeating. It also distills this entire game of carbohydrates into three essential bullet points. And here they are:

To obtain sustained energy and also boost your weight loss efforts, we only have to focus on three main factors:

1. Regulating our blood sugars
2. Stabilizing our insulin response
3. Mitigating inflammation in our body

That's it. Now, let me give you a quick, actionable strategy that will help you do this in a way that delivers results you can see and feel almost *immediately*.

Enter a concept known as "carb optimization."

Carb optimization basically involves going back and forth between high-carb days and low-carb days.

Having a carb rotation ritual in your diet can be an effective way to keep sustained energy levels and boost your weight loss efforts. It's a good way to replenish your glycogen stores for when your body needs it, but it also allows you to burn more fat for energy, which is ideal for losing weight.

Let me give you two simple carb optimization methods you can use:

Carb Optimization Method No. 1: Daily Progression

The Daily Progression method of carb optimization is simply starting off your week with a low amount of carbs and then gradually increasing them as the week progresses.

This is what I recommend to my clients. Why? It's because when you start your week with low-carb days, then gradually progress to moderate levels of carbs in the middle of the week, and then finish with higher carb days on the weekend, you'll be giving yourself the best chance to maximize your energy levels when you need to be most productive.

Here's what an ideal schedule should look like to optimize your body and mind:

Monday: Low carb	(50-100g)
Tuesday: Low carb	(50-100g)
Wednesday: Moderate carb	(100-150g)
Thursday: Low carb	(50-100g)
Friday: Low carb	(50-100g)
Saturday: High carb	(150-200g)
Sunday: Low carb	(50-100g)

Here's an important thing to remember when optimizing your carb intake: Keep your fat intake lower on high-carb days and your carb intake lower on high-fat days. In other words, **don't combine high fat and high carbs on the same day. Nor do you want to combine low fat and low carb on the same day.**

Here's why: When you eat a high-carb meal, your body produces insulin, which helps to store the carbohydrates as glycogen in your muscles and liver. Fine, that's appropriate and good. *However,* whenever you eat high fat along with those high carbs, it becomes an overload. The fat can interfere with this carb storage process and cause the carbohydrates to be stored as fat instead, (which is exactly what you don't want).

Here's a quick summary:

- When you go "low and low" — low carb and low fat — you're depriving yourself of crucial nutrients and your energy levels will drop. Avoid this situation.
- When you go "high and high" — high carb and high

fat — it creates an unhealthy surplus and your body is forced to store fat exactly where you don't want it.

Think of it like this: Imagine your body is like a battery. Carbohydrates are like the electricity that charges the battery, and fats are like the reserve power. On high-carb days, you're charging your battery with carbohydrates to use as energy later, but on high-fat days, you're conserving power by relying more on stored fats. By alternating between high-carb and high-fat days, you're able to maintain a balance of charge in your battery and use the stored energy when you need it, without overloading the battery or running it down.

Finally, here's an easy way to execute this Daily Progression carb strategy: Tie it to your activity levels that day. If you have a very physically active day, then you can increase your level of eating carbohydrates. If you are having a more sedentary day, then eat a lower portion of your calories as carbs.

Think in terms of "earning your carbs."

Carb Optimization Method No. 2: Save Your Carbs for Later in the Day

One smart idea for you to consider is to forget about customizing the amount of carbohydrates you eat for each day of the week. Instead, simply eat the same ratio each day — *but save your carbs for later in the day.*

By saving your carbs for later in the day, you can avoid any potential insulin spikes and keep your energy levels stable throughout the day.

This means you'll be able to focus better, be more productive, and have the energy to tackle whatever the day throws at you.

Additionally, consuming carbohydrates at night can help to promote better sleep. When you consume carbs at night, it triggers the release of the hormone serotonin, which can make you feel calm and relaxed.

This can make it easier to fall asleep and get a better quality of sleep. Not only that, but serotonin is also known to help regulate appetite, which can make it easier to resist cravings and stick to your diet.

Overall, by saving your carbs for later in the day, (on the days you choose to consume them), you can maintain stable energy levels, promote better sleep, and support weight management.

What to Start With Right Now

To start feeling better immediately and begin raising your energy levels and drop fat, do the following:

1. Keep a food diary for one week to monitor what you're currently eating in general. Write down the amount of calories, along with the amount of carbohydrates and fats in grams. Learn to read labels, but don't worry about being super precise. If you have to guesstimate, do so. The idea is to simply get an idea of what is considered high and low carb, as well as what is low and high fat.

2. Next, pick one of the two carb optimization methods

described above: The Daily Progression method or simply saving your carbs for later in the day, regardless of the day of the week.

3. Never have a day where you eat **high** levels of ***both*** carbohydrates and fat.

4. Never have a day where you eat **low** levels of ***both*** carbohydrates and fat.

5. Follow the 90/10 rule: Aim to hit your weekly nutrition goals 90 percent of the time. Look, there's no reason to feel like you're missing out on the good stuff ALL the time. You can still meet your health goals and go off the rails a bit once in a while. *But only once in a while.* Just make sure you're getting back on track the next day and continuing to make progress. It's all about progress, not perfection! Don't beat yourself up if you slip up, just get back on track and keep moving forward.

Now that you have a better understanding of the types of carbohydrates that are best for you — and when to consume them and how to achieve balance through eating with the 90/10 rule — it's time to take it to the next level and *really* optimize your energy levels and body for optimal performance.

This next part really brings it all together. I'm excited for you! Let's keep going.

Step #3 Eat in Time-Restricted Windows

Do you want to know perhaps the biggest secret to this entire puzzle?

It relates to something I haven't yet discussed in detail. But I'm about to get into it now, and it's extremely exciting.

Before I give you the secret, let's talk about the one thing that absolutely *must* occur if you are to drop those pounds you're eager to shed.

And that one thing is restricting calories. Simply put, you must create a *calorie deficit* in order to lose weight.

Yeah, yeah, I know: Losing weight is more complicated than just "calories in, calories out," but it's also true that if you want to lose weight, you simply must find a way to create a calorie deficit on a consistent basis.

What would you say if I told you there was a super-simple way to reduce your calories that was effortless, eliminated all your cravings, and actually made you more productive to boot?

Time-restricted eating does all those things (and more, as you'll see in a minute).

This is the secret I hinted at earlier. It's also known as intermittent fasting, and there's a reason it has experienced a resurgence in the health and medical space in recent years.

Simply put, intermittent fasting is just what it sounds like: it's abstaining from calories for a period of time. You only eat during a specific window of time during your day.

Now, many people see the word "fasting" and immediately panic, thinking they will be starving themselves using this method. It's simply not true. In fact, using this eating strategy actually reduces hunger, believe it or not.

Also, don't confuse this style of eating with "liquid fasts." That's not what this is. With my plan, you actually get to eat *real food* — specifically food that is tasty, nutritious, and deeply satisfying.

I have found that many high-performing guys love the challenge of eating only during certain hours of the day. (However, after a while, the "challenge" part wears off because it becomes so easy- and it simply turns into your routine.)

Actor Hugh Jackman, for example, discovered this method of eating while preparing for his role in "The Wolverine." He became a vocal advocate for intermittent fasting and, well, the results speak for themselves.

Before I show you how to do it, take a look at the benefits of eating in time-restricted windows:

- **Consistent energy levels:** Instead of feeling like your body is running on empty after a big meal, you'll have a steady supply of fuel to power you through the day.
- **Improved insulin sensitivity:** Think of it as a "tune-up" for your body's insulin levels, which can

help keep your blood sugar in check and lower your risk of diabetes.

- **Increased fat burning:** When you're not constantly eating, your body will begin to burn stored fat for energy, like a car switching to a higher gear.
- **Boosted immunity:** By giving your body a break from constant digestion, you're allowing it to focus on "maintenance" functions like fighting off infection and illness.
- **Increased cell autophagy**, which is the process your body uses to "clean up" and recycle cells
- **A reduced risk of diabetes, cancer, and heart disease**
- **An increase in human growth hormone**, (which helps you increase energy, bone density, and muscle)
- **A reduction in inflammation and improved gut health**
- **Improved mental clarity and cognitive function**
- **It can even improve the health and appearance of your skin.**

Oh, and we haven't even gotten to the benefit of weight loss yet!

Here's the good news: By reducing your eating windows, it's much easier to generate and maintain an overall calorie deficit, which in turn, gives your body the chance to burn off excess "weight" (or fat) that might be slowing it down.

How can this simple act of timing your meals accomplish so much?

Well, just like a car needs regular tune-ups and maintenance to keep running at peak performance, your body needs a break from constant digestion to allow it to focus on other important functions.

By reducing your eating windows, you're giving your body the "pit stop" it needs to refuel and perform at its best.

What to Start with Right Now

Begin time-restricted eating with whatever method appeals to you most. Don't go extreme at first. You can always dial up your fasting window and keep in mind that **you will still experience many of the same benefits with "milder" versions.**

Three effective ways to do time-restricted eating:

Overnight Fasting

This version is super simple. You simply don't snack between dinner and bedtime, and then wait as long as is comfortable before having breakfast. **What you're shooting for here is a minimum of 12 hours.** This is pretty easy for most people and it still activates cell autophagy as well as the other benefits. However, this method doesn't maximize the advantages of fasting. If you're using fasting for weight loss, a smaller fasting window means more time to eat, and it may not help you decrease the number of calories you consume.

The 14-Hour Fast

This is easy for many because think about it — you'll be sleeping for eight of these hours anyway! (And if you're not getting eight hours of sleep, then go back and read Chapter 7.) For instance, if you finish your dinner by 7 p.m., then you simply wait until 9 a.m. the next morning for your first calories of the day.

The 16/8 Method

This one is a little more challenging. It's eating only during an eight-hour window during the day. For example, eat from 12 noon to 8 p.m. daily. If you are struggling to maintain your fast during those last few hours, here are some tips:

Of course, with any version you come up with, you can adjust these time frames to fit your schedule and lifestyle. Remember to consult with your healthcare professional before making any significant changes in your diet and lifestyle.

The bottom line: By eating within certain time windows, you can rev up your metabolism and keep your energy levels running smoothly throughout the day. Trust me, it's a game-changer!

Here are two other tips to use when using time-restricted eating:

1. **Aim for eating 2.5 meals each day.**

   This could look like:

   1. Main Meal #1 (break your fast around lunch)
      a. Middle Meal (small high-protein snack in mid-afternoon, if necessary)
   2. Main Meal #2 (dinner)

   Eventually, many guys who incorporate intermittent fasting end up eating only two meals — sometimes even just *one* meal. Why? It's because, as I mentioned earlier, eating this way actually *reduces* your appetite! You literally stop thinking about food all the time because your body learns to run on fat, and you no longer are at the whim of your insulin response, (which can get greedy if you keep feeding it). People who eat five to six meals per day are training their bodies to be almost continually hungry and that leads to an unproductive preoccupation with food. Intermittent fasting stops all that.

   This is one of the most exciting parts of eating this way: You simply stop thinking about food so much. You still retain all the pleasure of eating, but in between meals you're not obsessing over when you get to eat next. You remain satisfied for longer periods of time which, among other benefits, allows you to become way more productive and get significantly more work done.

2. **Consume only water, tea, or coffee (no milk or sugar) during your fast.**

I'm including this as a tip because it's a common question what one can, and cannot consume, during a fast. Basically, your goal is to consume zero calories. However, this leads to a common question: Will a splash of milk in your coffee break your fast? Many experts will tell you that if you drink something with less than 50 calories then your body will remain in the fasted state. I think this is a reasonable approach. So having a very small amount of milk, cream or zero calorie sweetener with your coffee is just fine. Tea should be no problem either. Just be aware that introducing calories of any kind can also become a slippery slope if you're not careful.

If you find yourself having trouble making it through the last couple hours of your fast, use these two strategies to complete your fast:

1. Get busy! Do something physical, even if it's just going for a walk. Find some sort of distraction during that last hour or so, and eventually, you will find it easier and easier to hit your fasting target.

2. Drink mineral water, or sparkling water, to tide you over. These can feel "heavier" or more "filling" than plain water and can make that last hour or two go much easier.

How to Navigate Nutrition While Eating On the Go

Finally, I felt this chapter wouldn't be complete without sharing with you how to navigate nutrition while you're eating on the go or going out for lunch or dinner. Feasting on the go or dining out shouldn't be a dietary disaster. That's why I've compiled my top suggestions for navigating nutrition while eating out.

Without further ado, let's dive into …

My Top Tips For Making Smart Choices When Dining Out

BREAKFAST STYLE RESTAURANTS:

Staying on track at diners, or any place that serves brunch, is pretty simple. Pick items from the menu that are high in protein but lower in carbs.

> **What to eat:** eggs, bacon, ham, and sausage. Frittatas and omelets are fantastic, (especially those with vegetables).
>
> **What to avoid:** Hash browns, pancakes (especially the syrup), bagels, orange juice, donuts.

FAST FOOD FRIED CHICKEN RESTAURANTS:

There's a single word you can use while ordering at a fast food fried chicken joint that will solve most of its nutritional downsides. And that word is… ***Grilled!***

Want a chicken sandwich? That's fine. But order it ***grilled***. By doing so, you'll skip all those evil trans fats by avoiding the deep fryer.

Want to go one better? Order the sandwich grilled, and tell them to serve it "open faced," meaning you'll get half the amount of bread. Even better, ditch the bun entirely!

Here are some more ordering tips to stay healthy:

- Order a grilled chicken salad but hold off on the dressing. Or at least order the dressing on the side.
- Ordering chicken tenders or nuggets? Order them, you guessed it, grilled.
- Consider ordering a rotisserie chicken because it's not breaded and fried.
- Skip the fries. Order a side of veggies instead.
- Skip the heavy carb sides completely, such as potatoes and biscuits.

FAST FOOD BURGER RESTAURANTS

Getting a low-carb burger is fortunately quite simple these days.

Here's how:

- Ask them to swap out the bun for a lettuce shell (also known as a "lettuce wrap"). Many, if not most, places offer this option now! It's surprisingly terrific! They usually use iceberg lettuce, which isn't exactly nutritionally dense, but if you've never had it, it's way more satisfying than you would guess. Not to mention you've just done yourself a huge favor by eliminating almost all carbs while avoiding all the downsides that come with white bread.

- Many burger places also let you opt for a grilled chicken salad or some grilled chicken tenders.
- Skip the fries, shakes, and any extra "pure junky greatness" for now.

MEXICAN RESTAURANTS

Entrees like fajitas are great and are high in protein. You can also aim to have a steak, chicken, or shrimp salad, but try to avoid the fried shell. There are plenty of other high-protein dishes you can get by adding in chicken, steak, or shrimp with salsa and veggies. However, hold off on the rice, beans, and extra round of chips. If it's a fast-food style Mexican restaurant, you can usually get a bowl that's loaded with protein.

What to eat: Protein such as chicken, beef, carnitas, steak, greens, fajita-style veggies.

What to avoid or minimize: Chips, shells, tortilla. Eat beans in moderation.

PIZZA RESTAURANTS

Pizza is the food that perhaps best represents the classic mistake of having high fat (cheese) and high carbs (crust) in the same meal. That combo goes straight to your midsection. You want to avoid this situation as much as possible. Honestly, if you're interested in dropping weight and replacing that dad bod with something more athletic, then avoid pizza altogether. Or, enjoy it maybe once per month as a rare treat.

If you find yourself at a pizza restaurant because of a business meeting or family event, then look for a salad option. Most places will offer an alternative like that (and get your dressing on the side!).

What to eat: Limited slices, thin crust wherever possible. Salads (dressing on the side), wings (and go easy on the dipping sauce)

What not to eat: The pizza! (Pretty much not kidding, see the explanation above). Mozzarella cheese sticks

CHINESE RESTAURANTS

If you're ordering out any style of Chinese food, aim to order a steamed chicken, steak, or shrimp dish with veggies. Any kind of steamed fish dish will be fine as well, and you can add on a vegetable soup to go with it.

Be aware that most Chinese dishes with lots of sauces are high carb and high fat. And when you mix high carb and high fat together, (most fast food options), that's a surefire way to add on the extra weight around the waistline as well as increase cholesterol.

STEAKHOUSES AND GRILLS

These are some of the easiest places to stay on track.

Why? It's simple: Most options are super high in protein.

What to eat: Any style of steak or meat you want. Simple veggies as a side dish.

What not to eat: Bread, fully loaded baked potato, dessert

ITALIAN RESTAURANTS

What to eat: Any fresh fish dish, lean-cut steak, grilled calamari or mussels, salads, veal, or any chicken dish that doesn't have loads of extra sauce

What not to eat: Pasta, bread, bread sticks, etc. Having a small side of pasta is perfectly fine if you are enjoying one of the protein-based choices you see in the "What to eat" section above. (But I do mean small!)

HAWAIIAN STYLE RESTAURANTS

Hawaiian cuisine, like poke bowls, can be a great choice as they are loaded with protein such as grilled chicken, salmon, tuna, pork, and/or beef. Just be mindful of all the extra toppings.

GREEK

What to eat: There are plenty of grilled options to

go for at a Greek style restaurant. Things like grilled chicken, steak, or lamb are great options to choose from. You can also opt for fresh fish, scallops, vegetables, and salads.

What not to eat: Bread and oil dipping sauces

AIRPORTS & GAS STATIONS

If you find yourself in between flights or on the road and starting to get hungry, I have good news: You *can* continue eating healthy, and it's easier than you might realize. Just follow these tips:

- Try to eat a full meal before you travel so that you're not arriving at the airport hungry in the first place.
- Opt for things like low-carb (low sugar) protein bars or drinks.
- Look for bags of nuts like almonds or cashews. Most bags of mixed nuts will work just fine. A small serving of fruit can be another option to grab as well.
- Avoid the free packaged snacks they often hand out during flights.
- Skip the candy bars, potato chips, and sugary sodas/energy drinks.
- Overall, keep it light until you're able to grab some real food at a different point in the day.

One Final Note About This All-Important Topic of Nutrition...

I hope you read this chapter carefully and took it seriously. I say that because it's all too easy to dismiss information on a topic that you've probably heard a lot about before. Fighting misinformation and clarifying key concepts were two of my highest priorities here. But most importantly, showing you how to get results... quickly.

Let me assure you — this issue of what you put into your body (and when) is super critical if you want to recapture the same energy you had in your twenties.

It's not only possible... it's inevitable- if you simply execute on some very simple concepts. And you will see and feel positive results almost immediately.

However, I want to be real about something...

Let's be honest: It can be challenging to make the right food choices consistently, especially if you're not exactly sure how to fit this new protocol into your busy lifestyle and tailor it to your specific needs and goals.

Also, implementing any eating strategy can feel like trying to change the oil in your car: It might seem simple enough, but if you're not exactly sure what you're doing, you could end up causing more harm than good.

That's where my Accelerated Method coaching program comes in. It's where this nutrition protocol is customized in a way that fits your specific needs, lifestyle factors, and goals.

Part of my customized plan is a simple-to-follow system known as "Feast Like A King." This is a set of simple, yet flexible nutrition principles tailored to fit your goals and lifestyle factors. They allow you to eat full, satisfying meals and eat the foods you truly enjoy without the worry of having to give up your social life because one dinner or drink will derail all your hard work and progress.

Here's how my client Dusty described it: "When I told my wife I had joined, she was happy for me, but a little nervous as she thought I'd have to deprive myself or jeopardize family dinners because of some 'strict' diet. But that hasn't been the case at all. In fact, she loves it! We're eating like kings!"

If this sounds good to you, and if you want to take the guesswork out of nutrition and have a customized approach that fits your lifestyle and helps you meet your health and fitness goals, visit *www.acceleratedmethod.com/call* and book a free chat to learn more.

Key Chapter Takeaways

- Understand that in order to obtain sustained energy and boost your weight loss efforts, we must focus on three main factors:

    1. Regulating our blood sugars
    2. Stabilizing our insulin response
    3. Mitigating inflammation in our body

- Start replacing unhealthy options like sugar and gluten with nutrient-dense choices like lean protein, healthy fats, and fibrous vegetables.

- Be strategic about your carb intake and timing. Follow one of the methods described in this chapter that best suits you.

- Eat in time-restricted windows. Follow the style of time-restricted eating that appeals to you most.

CASE STUDY

Andy M., North Carolina, High-Level Executive

From Burned Out and Exhausted to Energized and Engaged: Andy's Journey to Optimal Health and Happiness

"Before, I was burning the candle at both ends that left very little time in my personal life. I'm talking about spending time with family, with my kids, not having the energy to get through the day, etc. Two and a half months ago I was burned out by 2:15 in the afternoon and ready to take a nap- and felt terrible. By the time I would get home in the evenings, I would lay down on the couch and find myself falling asleep at 8:15 in the evening.

I'd get home and my kids would want to play — they'd want to shoot hoops in the driveway, kick a soccer ball on the grass, throw a football and I just flat out didn't have the energy for it. I came to realize I'm shortchanging not only my kids' lives but also my own.

I realized what I was sacrificing on the personal side was taking more of a toll that I wasn't willing to pay any longer. Now, I feel better overall, I have a ton more energy. I'm able to spend as much time with my kids as they want me to spend. A full 10 weeks into the program, I am down 28 pounds. I'm down inches everywhere. From my neck, shoulders, chest, waist and hips- multiple inches. Clothes fit better. I keep punching holes in a belt that I have worn for 11 or 12 years, and one of these days, I'm going to run out of a room. I sleep better. I wake up supercharged. I get my day started, I know what to expect. It's been fantastic for me."

— Andy M., North Carolina, High-Level Executive

CHAPTER 9

Movement and Training Secrets to Achieve Peak Health, Defy Aging, and Ditch the "Dad Bod" Forever

Rad Bod or Dad Bod?

The question of "Rad Bod or Dad Bod" was brought to the forefront on a segment of the James Corden show, where Mark Wahlberg was challenged to guess which men had dad bods and which had rad bods based solely on their facial appearances.

While it was all in good fun, it reminded me of something I had read in the news a couple of years back, claiming that "men with dad bods show signs of having more confidence."

But, as someone who has been there, I call BS.

I can tell you that during my own dad bod days, I only felt out of shape and exhausted. The only confidence I had was fake and usually "created" after a couple of drinks.

I've also worked with countless men who told me the same thing. Despite their take-charge attitude in the workplace, deep down they had rock bottom confidence when they were out of shape.

They avoided going on family vacations. Or, when they *did* go, they dreaded it because even the thought of taking their shirt off at the pool or beach was just pure embarrassment.

They avoided long pauses in front of the mirror. They wore oversize shirts in order to hide their beer guts as much as possible. And they avoided being intimate with their wife or significant other because they didn't feel as desirable as they once were.

Maybe you can relate?

If so, I get it.

As a busy man, I know all too well the struggles of trying to balance work, family, and personal responsibilities.

It can be easy to let our physical health slip to the bottom of the priority list.

But here's the thing — as a busy man, especially if you're a dad, don't you owe it to yourself and your loved ones to take care of your body?

Don't you owe it to your kids to be a role model of healthy living and to show them how to live life with energy and passion?

And even if you're not a dad, but you're a husband or you're in a relationship...

Don't you owe it to your wife or significant other to show up as the fit, energetic, and desirable you?

Additionally, as a high performer, don't you owe it to those you lead on the work front to lead yourself?

How can they trust you to lead them otherwise?

Being a high performer means being a leader ... leading by example ... and taking care of your physical health is a key aspect of leading yourself effectively.

It's not just about looking good. It's about feeling good and being the best version of yourself for those around you.

And it's also about equipping you with all the efficient movements and training secrets you need to achieve peak health, defy aging, and ditch the dad bod forever.

Before I get into what to do next, let's take care of one of the biggest mistakes men make that can derail them before they even get started.

The Chronic Cardio Conundrum

Many men believe that in order to achieve peak health and shed the "dad bod," they need to engage in non stop cardio.

They'll put on their running shoes and rack up endless miles, or stare at their smartwatch obsessively trying to close those activity rings, only to realize it's not leading to the results they were hoping for.

They'll fork over a small fortune for those hyped-up cardio gyms that give them a shiny gadget to wear, but with little to no results to show for it. Or they'll drop a ton of cash on that at-home cycling bike, only to end up using it as a clothing rack, a useless monument that gave them nothing more than disappointment and a sore ass.

If this describes you, I feel your pain. And I'm here to tell you it's not your fault. This topic might be the single biggest source of misinformation and wasted effort in the history of fitness.

Listen up, engaging in chronic cardio, especially as a high-performing man, can be a recipe for disaster.

Not only will you be left with little to show for all your hard work, but it can also lead to a whole host of negative side effects.

First off, it's easy to feel like a hamster on a wheel, going nowhere fast. You'll be running in circles, racking up miles and zone minutes, but your waistline and energy levels won't budge.

Next, you'll start to feel like your joints are being used as chew toys by a pack of rabid dogs. Constant pounding on the pavement or a plastic machine can take a toll on your joints, leaving you feeling sore and stiff.

And let's not forget the boredom factor. Running on the treadmill for hours on end can make even the most interesting person feel like they're losing their mind.

But perhaps the worst part of all is that chronic cardio can lead to a decrease in lean muscle tissue, which can make you look flaccid, feel weak, and leave you with less energy.

It's like trying to put out a fire with gasoline; you're just making things worse.

And let's not forget about your stress hormone, cortisol. It's probably already skyrocketing due to the stress you face in everyday life, which of course causes you to gain weight and feel drained in the first place.

Well, guess what?

Engaging in chronic cardio can lead to an excessive *increase* in cortisol levels. This is because cardio, especially at high intensities, can trigger the release of cortisol as a response to the stress of intense physical activity. And if you're already stressed out trying to manage all the other obligations in your busy life, this can wreak havoc on your body.

Chronic cardio is like trying to win a game with only one strategy; you might get lucky once or twice, but eventually your opponents will catch on and you'll lose. It's a one-dimensional approach that can lead to negative side effects and an utter lack of progress. This of course leads to disappointment and, worst of all, quitting on your dreams of becoming fit.

My clients are often surprised at the results they get without doing "dedicated" cardio like running or cycling. The type of training I recommend — what you're about to discover in a minute — is more like "muscle building cardio" that combines the best of both worlds. It helps you get lean and mean while also getting your heart pumping and improving your cardiovascular health.

Now, don't get me wrong. I'm not completely anti-cardio. In fact, I'm a big fan of incorporating things like walking, short sprints, swimming, or even something like the occasional game of pickup basketball to achieve a good fitness balance.

But here's the real secret to winning the battle against the "dad bod" and achieving peak health: **adding resistance training to the mix.**

For some unknown reason, resistance training is still too often overlooked!

After reading this chapter, that won't be an issue for you. Let's get to it!

Unlocking the Power of Resistance Training for a Leaner, Stronger, Younger You

You're about to say goodbye to the "dad bod" and hello to a leaner, stronger, more youthful version of yourself with resistance training.

A quick definition of terms before we start:

Resistance training is any type of exercise that uses resistance to challenge your muscles. This can include using free weights, weight machines, or even just your own bodyweight. The goal is to push your muscles to work harder than they're used to by increasing time under tension, (the amount of time a muscle is under strain during a set of resistance exercise), which helps them grow stronger and more toned over time.

You probably knew all that. But what you might *not* have known is that, unlike chronic cardio — which is like a one-hit wonder at a karaoke bar — resistance training remains the true rockstar of workouts. It's like the Bruce Springsteen of exercise — it just keeps on rocking long after the show is over.

You see, resistance training not only burns calories during the workout, but it also helps to increase lean muscle tissue, which in turn boosts your metabolism. Which means you're burning additional calories long after your workout is over, even when you're just sitting at your desk or watching the game.

One study, published in the *Journal of Strength and Conditioning Research* in 2016, found that after 12 weeks of resistance training, participants increased their metabolic rate by 7 percent, compared to a 1 percent increase in those who did only cardio.

That's huge. By increasing your metabolic rate, you'll not only shed those extra pounds around the midsection, but you'll also have a leaner, more toned body composition overall.

But it's not just about the aesthetics. Resistance training is akin to the fountain of youth for your body. It can improve bone density, which can help prevent osteoporosis, reduce the risk of falls, lower the risk of chronic diseases, and boost your mood and mental focus. It can also protect against sarcopenia, the age-related loss of lean muscle and strength.

That's quite a payoff! But I want to say something more about sarcopenia here because it's a serious condition that can significantly impact a person's quality of life.

Sarcopenia can be compared to a bank account that is not regularly contributed to. Just like how a bank account that doesn't receive regular deposits will dwindle, our muscles also suffer from a lack of maintenance and use. As we age and become less active, the "deposits" of lean muscle and strength gradually decrease, leading to a decline in overall physical function and an increased risk of injury.

But the good news is that just like a bank account can be replenished through regular deposits, our muscles can also be maintained and strengthened through regular resistance training exercises.

This doesn't happen by itself, of course. In order to prevent your muscles from becoming the physical equivalent of a broke retiree, you need to make some regular weightlifting deposits, or engage in some other forms of resistance training.

Oh and I almost forgot...

Want to stay sharp, focused, and on top of your game?

Well, with resistance training, you'll be boosting your BDNF (Brain-Derived Neurotrophic Factor) levels, the superhero protein that helps keep your brain cells strong, improving blood flow to the brain, which in turn gives you more energy, focus and also helps you to stay calm under pressure.

It's like a one-stop shop for maintaining both a strong body and a sharp mind.

In short, resistance training really IS the secret weapon for ditching the dad bod for good, looking 10 years younger, and staying on top of your game. It's truly the ultimate multi-tasker for peak health.

With that in mind, let me tell you a quick story that my former client Shaun shared with me.

Shaun is someone who shed more than 60 pounds with my help. He worked hard and gained a ton of energy in the process. He told me a story about a friend who practically serves as a public service announcement for anyone who doubts the power of resistance training.

His friend, let's call him "Dad Bod Dave," was tired of feeling sluggish and the few extra pounds that came along with it.

So one day, Dave decided it was time to take control of his health and start his journey to a better version of himself.

At first, progress was slow. But eventually, the compliments started pouring in. People noticed that Dave was losing weight.

But as time went on, something strange happened.

Dave's weight loss permanently plateaued. Despite his

continued efforts, his remaining stubborn belly fat just wouldn't budge. Even worse, he also noticed that his energy levels began dropping unexpectedly. And after his previous gains, he now looked flaccid, despite the previous weight loss.

This left him feeling deflated. He remained hesitant to take his shirt off around others.

The reason for this reversal of fortune? Dave had become addicted to cardio. He had been neglecting resistance training.

His problem was a common one, something I see over and over: Dave was so focused on that number on the scale, he became unwilling to lift weights for fear it would make him gain weight and bulk up.

Dave had bought into one of the most pervasive myths in fitness. He didn't know the truth, that resistance training is the key to melting away fat. Just like a sculptor chips away at a block of marble to reveal a masterpiece, resistance training chisels away at the body to reveal a lean and mean body that turns heads.

Moral of the story? Don't be like Dave. If you want to ditch the dad bod, resistance training is non-negotiable.

Efficiency Without Excess: Smart Resistance Training That Won't Rob You of Precious Time or Leave You Feeling Like You've Been Hit By a Truck

Let's be real, as a busy high-performer, the thought of

spending endless hours working out or pushing yourself to exhaustion every day sounds like a nightmare.

But what if I told you that you can achieve peak health without sacrificing hours from your day or pushing yourself to the brink?

Allow me to introduce you to what I like to call:

"Efficiency-Driven Movement"

This is a training method that focuses on maximizing results in minimum time.

Think of efficiency-driven movement as a "power suit" for your body. It's the perfect workout for busy, high-performing men who want to look and feel their best without sacrificing all their time and energy.

Unlike traditional resistance training methods that leave you feeling like a "corporate drone" after a long day at the office, efficiency-driven movement is a low-impact style of training that keeps your heart rate elevated that will help you burn fat, build lean muscle, and boost energy levels without putting too much strain on your joints or leaves you feeling like you just got hit by a truck.

It's like a "business class workout" that will leave you feeling refreshed, not drained.

Efficiency-driven movement is perfect for busy men because it's quick and to the point. It can be done with a simple set of dumbbells or even your own bodyweight, making it flexible and customizable to fit your schedule.

To give you a clear visual of what efficiency driven movement looks like, here's a few examples of efficiency-driven resistance training workouts, using just your bodyweight and/or dumbbells only:

Sample 15-Minute Efficiency-Driven Workout — Bodyweight Only

1. Push-ups 12 reps
2. Renegade Rows 12 reps
3. Squats 12 reps
4. Lunges 12 reps (6 reps per leg)
5. Plank 30 seconds
6. Rest 30 seconds

Repeat the circuit hitting ***as many rounds as you can with as little rest as possible until the 15-minute timer goes off.***

Note: If you can't hit all the reps for certain exercises, aim to subtract 2 to 3 reps.

Sample 15-Minute Efficiency-Driven Workout — with Dumbbells

1. Dumbbell overhead press 12 reps
2. Dumbbell bent-over rows 12 reps
3. Dumbbell bicep curls 12 reps
4. Dumbbell tricep extension 12 reps
5. Dumbbell deadlifts 12 reps
6. Rest 30 seconds

Repeat the circuit hitting ***as many rounds as you can with as little rest as possible until the 15-minute timer goes off.***

Note: If you can't hit all the reps for certain exercises, aim to subtract 2 to 3 reps.

Frequency: How often should you do this workout?

Short answer: at least four times a week for best results.

Here's why, (along with some important, additional info):

For maximum results from these types of movement routines, it's essential to focus on proper technique and not rush through the exercises. Keeping a steady, controlled pace will ensure that you're getting the most out of each movement and will set you on the path to achieving peak health. It also means you won't be blasting your body so intensely that you'll need days to recover. Good! And that's why you should aim to incorporate these efficient-driven workouts at least four times a week for best results.

Would you like to take your resistance training to the next level? Then take a look at what I have for you next.

BONUS: The Accelerated Hybrid Routine: The 18-Minute Workout for Maximum Efficiency

If you would like an even better challenge, then use the bonus 18-minute efficiency driven hybrid workout below.

By combining both dumbbells and bodyweight exercises,

this routine offers a unique and challenging approach to resistance training.

Two Notes About the Workout Below:

1. To View How to Perform Each Exercise for this efficiency-driven movement framework, go to *www.acceleratedmethod.com/movement* to learn more.
2. If you don't have a pair of dumbbells- I invite you to do the alternative exercise that's provided next to each weighted exercise.

INSTRUCTIONS:	
Set your timer for 18 minutes. Once the timer begins, go through exercise 1 (A1) to exercise 5 (A5) as many rounds as possible with as little rest as possible until the 18 minute timer ends. **Note:** *If you can't hit all the reps for certain exercises, aim to subtract 2 to 3 reps.*	
A1	**Goblet Squats or Bodyweight Squats: Complete 10 Reps**
	Once you complete 10 reps, take a 25-second rest then proceed to the next exercise in this circuit *Pro tip: Go Slow on the Descend of Every Movement*

A2	**Flutter Kicks: Complete 15 Reps**
	Once you complete 15 Reps, take a 25 second rest then proceed to the next exercise in this circuit
A3	**Bodyweight Renegade Rows: Complete 10 Reps**
	Once you complete 10 Reps, take a 25 second rest then proceed to the next exercise in this circuit
A4	**Dumbbell Reverse Lunges or Bodyweight Reverse Lunges: Complete 10 Reps**
	Once you complete 10 Reps, take a 25 second rest then proceed to the next exercise in this circuit
A5	**Burpees: Complete Exercise for 30 seconds**
	Once you complete the 30 seconds for this exercise, take a 25 second rest then go back into the first exercise of this A Circuit. Keep Going through the circuit until the timer goes off

****To View How to Perform Each Exercise as well as see a few more examples of efficient-driven movement frameworks**, go to *www.acceleratedmethod.com/movement* to learn more

Some Caveats, Disclaimers, and Common Sense

I realize that putting exercise movements in a book like this won't be able to fit all guys equally. I did my best to design the above workouts to hit as broad a range as possible, but I know there are all sorts of special situations among readers. Let me cover some of them now, as well as answer some common questions.

Physical Limitations

If you have limitations that prevent you from being able to do resistance training, no problem! There are still many other things you can do, such as walking. (There's a reason the 10,000 steps protocol is so popular; it's quite effective.) For instance, you might remember my client Wayne from Chapter 3, who came into the program with such significant physical limitations that the only movement he could do at first was simply walking. Which was great — Wayne crushed his walking routine so consistently he earned the nickname, "The Step King."

Bottom line, no matter how many limitations you have — and even if you have none — always exercise within your limitations, don't push things beyond a reasonable range, and dial back the urge to "leave it all on the field." Feeling overly sore the next day doesn't mean you "killed it." It means you went overkill and possibly risked real harm to your body that was simply unnecessary.

"Beast Mode"-style workouts that leave you peeled off the floor and in pain for days aren't the smartest approach for a high performer like yourself when it comes to boosting energy and getting in great shape.

What you want instead are movement routines that are efficient, structured properly, not too time-consuming, and allow you to be *consistent*. You want routines that give you energy, not take it away.

I sincerely believe that any man who follows any of the workout protocols laid out in this chapter with intelligence and diligence will begin feeling better almost immediately. That means more energy, a stronger frame, increased confidence, and believe it or not, you'll actually start craving healthier foods without even trying.

Regardless of what routine you choose to do next, just remember, to keep MOVING in some capacity- and you'll be GOLDEN.

Get started and let me know how it goes for you.

Want These Workouts In Your Back Pocket Wherever You Go?

What I've laid out in this chapter can deliver real results for you, starting today.

There's just one problem I see all the time…

Here it is: Many, (if not most, guys), will find themselves literally *guessing* on what kind of movement or workouts they should be doing next. Which, of course, only wastes time and derails them from making any real progress if they don't guess correctly.

Your specific movement protocol should have the right number of exercises, volume amount, and intensity range that's specifically programmed to YOU — *your lifestyle,* and *your goals.*

If you want to shed those extra pounds and boost your energy, you need to mix things up.

Progressive overload is the secret ingredient to consistent progress. No matter how effective the movement routines are, our bodies eventually get accustomed to any training plan we follow.

This is one reason I created the Accelerated Hybrid Training System (AHTS).

This system is what my private clients use. The AHTS takes ***less than 30 minutes per day to implement.*** It's designed in a way that gives you energy and also increases metabolism over a 48-hour period, *even when you're not actively working out!*

This means you can stay in fat burning mode longer, which means lose more weight in less time … effortlessly.

My favorite feature of this private program is that everything is located at the tap of a finger on your smartphone, iPad, or any mobile device. It works like this: You simply open this app- and it's GO TIME. No fumbling around with spiral notebooks, printing out pages, or downloading PDFs — everything you need is just a tap away on your smartphone. You're shown what to do, step by step and move by move, without any guesswork whatsoever.

If you want to find out how to get access to this app and much more, then please visit *https://www.acceleratedmethod.com/call* to book in a chat with me or a member of my team.

Key Chapter Takeaways

- No matter how busy you are, you owe it to yourself and your loved ones to take care of your body.
- Being in great physical shape is not just about looking good. It's about feeling good and being the best version of yourself for those around you.
- Doing non stop "chronic cardio" increases cortisol levels and will work against your efforts to increase strength, gain energy, and get lean. Focus on efficiency-driven movements instead.
- The real secret to winning the battle against the "dad bod" and achieving peak health is adding resistance training to the mix.

- As the rockstar of physical fitness, resistance training increases your metabolic rate and allows your body to burn fat long after you have finished your workout. This leads to a leaner, more toned body composition.
- Follow the workouts in this chapter that are appropriate for you and never push things past what is comfortable. If you are significantly sore the next day, you did more harm than good and that will hinder your results.

CASE STUDY

Jose V., Seattle, WA, Aviation Specialist

"I feel completely different. I'm 45. But to be honest, inside, I now feel more like 25..."

"I was always just tired and exhausted. I could sleep eight hours, even nine hours or ten, and still wake up tired. And this would be every week, just a consistent drag. My daily routine consisted of three to five cups of coffee a day, one or two sodas a day, I would have a Red Bull here and there throughout the week. That's where my energy came from. But I would always just get home exhausted after work.

I just got to a point where I was just sick of being tired. It's not easy to say, but it affected everything. Not just where I work either. I just wasn't able to give it 100 percent with my closest friends and family. I just wasn't available to go and hang out with them, not during the week or even on the weekends.

What I can tell you is it's only been 10 weeks ... and in 10 weeks I do not feel that drag of being tired all the time. I actually wake up with energy. And I do not do coffee anymore.

Physically, I just feel better, my clothes fit better. I've dropped about 15 pounds. I feel completely different. I'm 45. But to be honest, inside, I now feel more like 25 because I feel energetic throughout the day. And that energy is real energy, it actually feels good, just to be energetic.

It feels good to wake up with energy, it feels good when I'm at work, and I have the energy. Throughout the day, and even after I go home from work, I'm no longer lounging on the couch, I actually can go out for a walk, and I actually now can go spend time with my family. I have that energy that I feel from morning to night. I have found what I had been looking for, which was that energy, that natural energy that I knew was inside."

— Jose V., Aviation Specialist in Seattle, WA

CHAPTER 10

The Productivity Boost: How to Maintain Mental Clarity, Focus, and Energy All Day Long

Welcome to the next level of unlocking your full potential.

Have you ever watched the movie "Limitless" with Bradley Cooper?

It's a story about a struggling writer who comes across a mysterious drug that unlocks the full potential of his brain, allowing him to achieve incredible success and wealth.

But what if I told you that this isn't just a Hollywood fantasy?

That, in fact, there are real-life strategies you can use to increase your mental clarity, focus, and energy, just like in the movie?

Now, I know what you might be thinking ...

"Oh great, another self-help book promising me the moon and the stars."

But hear me out on this.

This chapter is going to introduce you to some upgraded strategies to get you on the path to experiencing that "limitless" feeling and really get you firing on ALL cylinders.

We will briefly explore the world of mental edge enhancers, including what they are, how they work, and how to use them to your advantage. Additionally, we will discuss the effects of alcohol on physical and mental performance and how to use it in a way that doesn't completely crush your progress or performance.

So, if you're ready to start firing on all twelve cylinders like a high-performance Ferrari instead of a four cylinder Yugo, then buckle up because this is going to be a wild ride.

The Limitless Mind: Harnessing the Power of Mental Edge Enhancers

Are you feeling like you're not quite operating at peak performance lately? You're not alone.

As we age, our brain's ability to stay sharp and focused can start to decline. But what if I told you there's a way to give your brain the boost it needs to stay on top of your game?

Enter mental edge enhancers, also known as "cognitive enhancers" or "nootropics."

Now, before you roll your eyes and think of shady deals

in dark alleys, let me tell you that mental-edge enhancers come in both natural and synthetic forms. And, unlike the prescription drugs you may have already heard of, natural nootropics such as omega-3 fatty acids, caffeine, and certain amino acids, have minimal risks and have been used for centuries in traditional medicine.

We're going to start with something everyone is familiar with.

Amp Up Your Performance: Simple Changes to Make Your Caffeine Work Harder for You

Let's kick off this conversation by discussing the most widely consumed mental edge enhancer on the planet: **caffeine.**

This little wonder drug can be found in everything from your morning cup of joe to your afternoon energy drink.

Of course, many people rely on caffeine to get through the day, and most are guilty of abusing it. (Full disclosure: this used to be me!)

But what if I told you there's a better way?

And no, I'm not talking about giving up caffeine. I'm talking about a new way to use caffeine that won't leave you feeling jittery, anxious, or with a pounding headache.

A way to use caffeine that will provide you with steady, all-day energy, *without the crash.*

The key is to use caffeine *strategically.*

This means paying attention not just to how much caffeine you drink, but *when* you drink it. This can make a huge difference!

As I mentioned in an earlier chapter, waiting to ingest caffeine at least one to two hours after waking up will allow your body to produce and release cortisol naturally, which can help you feel more alert and awake throughout the day ensuring you bypass any afternoon crash.

With that in mind, it's also important to consider the right amount of caffeine to consume in any given period of time in order to maximize its effectiveness.

Small doses of caffeine are often more effective than large doses, as they can provide a steady level of energy throughout the day without the crash that often comes with consuming too much caffeine at once.

According to a study done by the US Army, consuming caffeine in smaller, more frequent doses throughout the day may result in better long-term focus.

The study involved a group of soldiers who were given either a placebo or a low dose of caffeine, (about the equivalent of one cup of coffee), at regular intervals throughout the beginning of the day. The soldiers who received the caffeine experienced a significant improvement in their ability to sustain attention and stay alert during a series of tasks that required prolonged periods of mental effort.

This suggests that rather than consuming all of your

caffeine at once, it may be more beneficial to spread your caffeine intake out over the course of the morning.

This may help to sustain focus and concentration for a longer period of time.

However, it's also important to note that consuming too much caffeine — even if spread out over time — can lead to negative side effects such as jitters, anxiety, and headaches.

So ... what's considered "too much" caffeine?

The answer can vary from person to person. While moderate consumption is generally recommended — no more than 400 mg per day for healthy adults — some studies suggest that even lower amounts of caffeine, such as 300mg per day, may lead to increased anxiety and jitters.

The "sweet spot" of caffeine dosage can vary from person to person.

My own experience is that 100 to 200 mg of caffeine spread out in small doses (25 to 50 milligrams) throughout the course of the morning can lead to a steady flow of sustained energy throughout the day.

Here's a list of common morning beverages to give you an idea of the caffeine content found in each beverage:

- Coffee (8 oz cup) : 95-200 mg
- Espresso (1 oz) : 63-100 mg
- Tea (8 oz cup) : 14-60 mg

- Black tea (8 oz cup) : 14-70 mg
- Green tea (8 oz cup) : 24-45 mg
- Matcha Tea (8 oz cup) 70-80 mg

Whether you see your favorite caffeinated drink listed or not, the important thing is that you know how much caffeine content is found in your morning beverage. From there, just be mindful to spread out the amount of caffeine you're consuming throughout the duration of the morning and not just take it down in one big hit.

The Power of Cycling Caffeine for Optimal Performance

Cycling your caffeine intake functions like a well-planned workout routine for your brain.

Just like how you wouldn't work out the same muscle group every day, you shouldn't be consuming caffeine every day.

By taking two to three days off a week, you are allowing your brain to recover and prevent it from getting too accustomed to caffeine. This way, when you do consume caffeine, it will have a stronger effect, similar to how a muscle works better after a rest day.

Consuming caffeine every day can lead to tolerance, where you need more and more caffeine to achieve the same effects. Of course, it can also lead to dependence, in which you could experience withdrawal symptoms such as headache and fatigue if you miss your daily dose.

By cycling your caffeine intake, you can prevent these negative effects and also give your body and mind a break, allowing them to recharge.

And look, I get it: You may feel like you can't miss even one day of coffee in the morning. But here's the thing: You don't have to! Simply ease into this method of caffeine cycling. You can start by cutting your caffeine in half on your "off" days, and then playing with it from there. Go as gradual as you want. For instance, maybe for two days a week you only drink three cups per day instead of five. And then a week or two later, those three cups become two... and then eventually just one. And then you'll be on the doorstep of being able to cut your caffeine to zero during a couple days per week, if you want.

Believe me, caffeine will take on a much more powerful effect when you do this! It's one of those things you simply have to experience to fully understand its power.

Bottom line, when you make the effort to be in control of your brain's performance, not the other way around, then cycling your caffeine intake can be a really effective strategy.

Next up, let's talk about the little-known secret weapon in winning the war against stress and burnout:

L-Theanine

Aside from utilizing caffeine strategically by limiting the quantity and dosage you have throughout the morning, adding L-theanine to your morning caffeinated beverage can help you experience a calm-like focus without any jitters.

L-Theanine is an amino acid found naturally in tea leaves, specifically in green and black tea. It is known for its calming and relaxing properties. L-Theanine works by increasing the activity of neurotransmitters, such as dopamine and GABA, that promote relaxation and reduce stress without causing drowsiness.

It also enhances the effects of caffeine, by counteracting the jittery and anxious side effects.

Adding L-Theanine to your morning cup of Joe or tea is like having a personal DJ for your brain. It harmoniously blends the stimulating effects of caffeine with a calming and relaxing melody, making your morning routine a symphony of productivity.

Another potent mental edge enhancer to step your game up is **L-Tyrosine**.

This powerful amino acid is like liquid gold for your brain. It will help boost your focus, sharpen your attention, and enhance your mental alertness. Think of it as a personal assistant for your gray matter, helping you power through the most demanding tasks of the day. And you can forget about that midday brain fog or afternoon slump; with L-Tyrosine, you'll be on top of your game all day long. It gives you the extra edge you need to conquer the day like a boss.

And finally, let me tell you about the ultimate mental

edge enhancer for high performers looking to stay sharp and focused:

Alpha-GPC

Alpha-GPC (Alpha-glycerylphosphorylcholine) is a powerful mental edge enhancer that has been shown to improve cognitive function by increasing levels of acetylcholine, a neurotransmitter that is vital for memory, learning, and focus. Think of it as the "gasoline" for your brain's engine, allowing it to run at peak performance. Not only does it help you stay alert and focused during the workday, but it also supports the growth of new brain cells and improves overall cognitive function. It is especially effective for high performers who are looking to maintain their edge in a busy and demanding environment. Imagine being able to navigate a crowded city street with ease. Alpha-GPC is like having a personal GPS for your brain, helping you stay on track and reach your destination with ease.

You can also find citicoline, the natural form of Alpha-GPC, in certain foods such as eggs, fish, (particularly salmon and cod), lean beef, and vegetables (like brussels sprouts and broccoli). Incorporating these foods into your nutrition protocol can also provide a natural boost to your cognitive function.

One final note: If you're wondering where to get these supplements, look no further than Amazon. While these supplements are indeed carried in various brick and mortar stores, Amazon is probably the quickest and easiest way to order them.

Let me tell you, these simple strategies to optimize your caffeine consumption can have a profound difference in your energy levels throughout the day. Many guys have been suffering the mid-afternoon slump for so long they think it's normal. It's not! Make the effort to incorporate these adjustments and say goodbye to brain fog, roller coaster energy rides, uncontrollable yawning late in the day ... and watch your mood and productivity soar as a result.

What to Start with Right Now

1. Wait at least 1-2 hours after waking up before consuming caffeine.

2. For sustained focus and concentration, caffeine should be consumed in smaller, more frequent doses throughout the morning time only. (As explained in chapter 7 on sleep- consider stopping caffeine consumption by 1 p.m. to avoid disruptions with sleep.)

3. Be aware of your caffeine tolerance, and consume caffeine in moderation. (Anywhere from 100-200 mg spread throughout the morning only, can typically provide a steady flow of energy all day long for most.)

4. Try cycling your caffeine and mental edge enhancers weekly by taking 2-3 days off per week to prevent tolerance and dependence.

5. Experiment with different caffeine sources and dosages to find what works best for you.

6. Read the label and keep track of your daily caffeine intake.

7. Consider adding L-Theanine to a morning caffeinated beverage to experience a calm-like focus without jitters.

8. Incorporate L-tyrosine to boost focus, attention, and mental alertness.

9. Look into Alpha-GPC as a powerful mental edge enhancer to improve cognitive function and support the growth of new brain cells.

10. Incorporate foods high in citicoline, such as eggs, fish, lean beef, and vegetables into your nutrition to provide a natural boost to cognitive function.

It is important to note that mental edge enhancers can have different effects on different people, and the optimal dosage can also vary from person to person. It is important to note that overconsumption of these substances can have negative effects on mental and physical health. As always, it is important to consult with a healthcare professional before making any changes to your diet or supplement regimen, especially if you are currently taking any medications, to ensure that the supplements and caffeine are safe for you to use in conjunction with your current medications. And be aware that the opposite of a mental edge enhancer would be a substance that impairs cognitive function such as sedatives, depressants, and psychoactive drugs.

Alcohol: The Insidious Menace Hiding in Plain Sight

Now that we've covered the ins and outs of mental edge enhancers and how to use them strategically for sustained energy, mental clarity, and focus, let's talk about a widely consumed mental edge *suppressor* that can have a detrimental effect on your physical and mental performance: **alcohol.**

Sure, a drink or two may help you relax and "take the edge off" after a long day, but consistently drinking alcohol, even in moderate amounts, can do a number on your energy, mental clarity, and focus. Not to mention the fact that it can make it even more challenging to drop extra weight.

Let me explain.

First, never forget that alcohol is a central nervous system depressant, which means it slows down brain function. This can lead to feelings of drowsiness and fatigue, making it harder to stay alert and focused throughout the day. Additionally, alcohol can disrupt the quality of your sleep, leading to a less restful sleep and waking up feeling groggy and unrested.

Alcohol also affects the balance of hormones in the body, specifically increasing the levels of cortisol and decreasing the levels of testosterone. High cortisol levels can lead to feelings of stress and anxiety, while low testosterone levels can lead to decreased energy, mood swings, and lack of focus.

Furthermore, alcohol can also make it harder for you to drop extra weight. Alcohol contains empty calories and can disrupt the balance of hormones that regulate hunger and metabolism. Additionally, as anyone who has found themselves at a Mexican food takeout window at 1 a.m. can tell you, drinking alcohol can lead to poor food choices and overeating, which can contribute to weight gain.

And let's not forget the dreaded hangover. A hangover is not just a headache and feeling tired, it can also include symptoms such as nausea, sensitivity to light and sound, and just generally feeling like shit. These symptoms can last for several hours, and in some cases, even into the next day.

Now, don't get it twisted. I'm not telling you that you can never drink alcohol again. It can be enjoyed in moderation and can be a great social lubricant and mood booster. But if you want to maintain high energy levels, mental clarity, and focus — and also lose those love handles in the process — then it's important to be mindful of how much, and how often, you're consuming it.

What's considered "moderation?"

Let's talk about moderation and what it means for you. The truth is, moderation is different for everyone. It's about finding that sweet spot between enjoying yourself and not overdoing it.

To find your personal sweet spot, ask yourself these two key questions:

Question No. 1: How much is too much?

Now look, I could sit here and write in stone the amount of drinks that you "*should*" have. That's what a doctor might do. But I'm not going to do that. For starters, I don't know what that number is... ***for YOU***. Putting a hard number on that is too simplistic. I don't believe the same answer applies to everyone. That's why I want **YOU** to ask yourself the question, "How much is too much?"

And look, I get that this might feel uncomfortable at first. But doing this will help start a self-reflection process that will lead you naturally to the right amount that works for you. If you want to be at your best and get back to being "the old you," then engaging in this process is hugely important.

So here's what I recommend to establish a safe and healthy moderation level for alcohol consumption: Set a general guideline for yourself by determining the maximum number of drinks you will have per week.

For example, you could start by setting a limit of having no more than one drink per day. Or, to really boost mental clarity, focus, and brain power during the week, you could consider saving those couple of drinks for the weekends only. Keep track of your alcohol consumption by using an app or writing it down in a journal and evaluate if you're staying within your established limit.

Question No. 2: How does alcohol make you feel?

Take the time to reflect on your emotional relationship to alcohol and how it affects your mood and well-being. Consider specific emotions you feel after drinking, such as anxiety, sadness, or regret, and how they impact your daily life.

Don't just give these questions mere superficial consideration. Really dig into them a bit. This self-reflection will pay off big-time if you take it seriously. This is your life after all, and it's not going to change itself without real effort and a little bit of contemplation.

So ask yourself: Do these negative emotions occur frequently after drinking even a small amount of alcohol in certain situations? To gain a deeper understanding of your relationship with alcohol, try keeping a journal where you write down your thoughts and feelings after each drink. Over time, you may see patterns or triggers that can help you make more informed decisions. You can also consider alternative activities or methods of managing stress or negative emotions, such as exercise, box-breathing, or spending time with friends and family.

Bottom line, finding the right balance is key to maintaining good health and feeling great. It's all about being mindful of how much and how often you're consuming alcohol, and being honest with yourself about how it makes you feel. It's all about finding that sweet spot that works for you.

Navigating the Fine Line:

How do you know when you've crossed the line between enjoying a drink or two as part of a healthy lifestyle and when it's becoming a problem? It can be tricky, but here are a few things to consider:

- If the thought of giving up alcohol even for a short time fills you with dread, consider that a red flag.
- Take a closer look at your relationship with alcohol. Ask yourself questions such as: Is alcohol an important part of my lifestyle? Why? What am I using alcohol for? Does it feel uncomfortable to not drink? Why?
- Set some guidelines for yourself. What's a reasonable amount for you to drink? How often per day, week or month? When is it smart for you to drink and when is it smarter for you to not drink?
- Pay attention to the way alcohol affects your other habits, like eating. Is there a relationship between your drinking and your food choices?
- Be mindful of the signals your body is sending you. Are there other issues that you've been avoiding that alcohol might be masking?

By being honest with yourself and paying attention to the way alcohol affects you, you'll be better equipped to navigate the fine line between enjoying a drink and having a problem.

Aside from experiencing low energy, poor focus, and

getting in the way of your weight loss efforts, here's a list of some other risks associated with moderate to heavy alcohol consumption:

1. Increased risk of liver disease, such as cirrhosis and liver cancer
2. Increased risk of pancreatitis
3. Increased risk of high blood pressure, heart disease, and stroke
4. Increased risk of certain types of cancer, such as breast, colon, and liver cancer
5. Increased risk of depression and anxiety
6. Increased risk of cognitive decline and dementia
7. Increased risk of sexual dysfunction
8. Increased risk of poor immune function

Here's my point: When it comes to drinking, make sure it's adding *value and pleasure* to your life. Not out of habit because you're feeling stressed, or simply because you don't want to drink alone.

Here's a question to ask yourself next time you're reaching for a drink: Is this truly adding value to my life ... or am I just going through the motions?

It's not just about being "healthy" or "unhealthy." It's about understanding the trade-offs you're making. Keep in mind that alcohol consumption is only one piece of the puzzle when it comes to maintaining high physical and mental performance. To decide whether or not to continue or cut back on drinking, it depends on the amount of alcohol you consume, your goals, and how you prioritize those things. Ultimately, it's up to you to decide what trade-offs you're willing to make.

The answer to drink may be as straightforward as: **Yes or No.**

Here's what I mean:

Saying "yes" for a highly productive week may mean saying "no" to alcohol throughout the week.

Saying "yes" to a defined and toned midsection may mean saying "no" to a few drinks on a night out.

Saying "yes" to better sleep, focus, and mood may mean saying "no" to your daily or every other night wine/beer/cocktail with dinner.

Saying "yes" to being a patient, present, and less reactive leader may mean saying "no" to the after work happy hour.

The key is to pay close attention to your drinking behaviors, gather data, and assess how alcohol serves or does not serve your well-being.

What to Start with Right Now

1. Be mindful of how much and how often you're consuming alcohol, as it can have negative effects on energy, mental clarity, focus, and weight loss.

2. Determine your personal moderation level by setting a general guideline, such as less than three drinks per week, then reflecting on how alcohol makes you feel emotionally.

3. Consider red flags in your relationship with alcohol, such as feeling dread at the thought of giving it up or using it as a crutch.

4. Set guidelines for yourself, including how much and how often you drink, when to say "yes" and when to say "no" to drinking, and pay attention to how alcohol affects other habits such as eating.

Aside from really dialing in the foundational principles that you've learned so far in this book — especially sleep and nutrition — deploying the mental enhancement strategies in this chapter can be extremely powerful tools in helping you to get back to feeling like you did back in your twenties. Don't dismiss them! (And no, I'm not talking about Twentysomething-Hangover Guy, I'm talking about Twentysomething- Go All Day and Night Guy.)

This is obviously a huge topic. And this book only has room for so much information. (For starters, entire books are written on the subjects of sleep, caffeine, alcohol, and nootropics alone.) However, if you're interested in hearing about some of the advanced-level supplementation and mental edge enhancement strategies I use for my high-level coaching clients, you can learn more by going here: *www.acceleratedmethod.com/call*

Key Chapter Takeaways

- Mental edge enhancers, also known as cognitive enhancers or nootropics, can help boost brain performance.
- Consuming caffeine 1-2 hours after waking up and in small, frequent doses throughout the morning can maximize its effectiveness.
- Cycling caffeine intake, and taking 2 to 3 days off a week, can prevent tolerance and dependence.
- Incorporating Mental Edge Enhancers like L-Theanine, L-Tyrosine, or Alpha-GPC into your morning routine can help improve cognitive function, reduce stress, and enhance focus and alertness.
- Alcohol is a central nervous system depressant that can negatively impact energy, mental clarity, and focus.
- Alcohol affects hormone balance and can lead to increased stress, decreased energy, and weight gain.
- Moderation is the key to consuming alcohol while still maintaining physical and mental health.
- To determine a safe and healthy moderation level, consider setting a general guideline for maximum drinks per week and reflect

on the emotional impact of alcohol on your mood and well-being.

- A self-reflection process, involving a journal to track alcohol consumption and emotions, can help determine patterns and make more informed decisions.

CASE STUDY

Kenny T., Texas, Business Owner

"I'm back to being a Ferrari ..."

"I was just feeling rundown and wasn't hitting on all cylinders. I wasn't the person I knew I could be, that I used to be. Just procrastinating a lot more often and didn't have the drive that I knew that was in me that I had before. I knew I needed to figure something out. I wasn't as available for my family, my wife and kids, and grandkids.

What brought me to the program was reading through it, doing research on it, and understanding that making this step was for myself. I'm down 25 pounds. The energy level and the drive factor of it, that's probably the biggest thing that I'm happy with and pleased with because I want to get out there again and do the stuff and do what I do. Because I enjoy it. There's no more just sitting back and not doing it. It's put me back into hitting on all 12 cylinders. I'm no longer the Yugo, I'm back to being a Ferrari."

— Kenny T., Texas, Business Owner

PART 3

Fanning the Flames for Momentum, Consistency, and Lasting Change

CHAPTER 11

Putting an End to the Stop-Start Cycle: Mastering the Art of Consistency

Any type of change can be difficult. Anything new can feel risky. Our minds (and egos) want to play it safe. But as high achievers, we don't play small. We play to win.

Except when it comes to our own health. Our health ends up at the bottom of the priority list time and time again. How many times have you started and stopped a fitness program?

Maybe you were on a winning streak with your consistency and then, out of nowhere, an event occurred. The weekend hits, kids get sick, you miss a couple days of your routine, projects pick up at work, the "honey-do list" gets a hold of you...whatever it is, the event happens and you stop staying consistent.

After that event occurs, you may think, "Well, I deserve a break." Or you turn to food or alcohol to relieve stress, thinking, "It wasn't that bad before..."

These justifications create a false lift to make you feel

better at the time, but they ultimately cause you to stop doing what you set out to do. You're then stuck in the constant loop of starting over and over again.

Does any of this sound familiar to you? Good! Because this chapter is all about breaking that cycle. In many ways, this might be the most important chapter in this book. I say this because none of the action-oriented steps we've already discussed — nutrition, exercise, hormones, a good morning routine, sleep, etc — none of those will matter a whit if you quit after just "giving it a try."

If you have ever been excited about embarking on a self-improvement journey... but then bailed on it for whatever reason, then you need to take every word in this chapter to heart.

Let's be honest. Creating time to exercise is hard, and eliminating all of the foods you love is tough, but the worst part is going to battle with your brain and your mindset. Your head will psych you out before anything else will. So, what gives?

If you can go after those huge projects and clients at work, or build a business from the ground up, or hit high sales goals over and over, why can't you achieve the same level of success with your health?

Well... you CAN. It just takes an understanding of the psychology behind change and how we can get derailed.

The Emotional Cycle of Change

Psychologists Don Kelley and Daryl Connor introduced their Emotional Cycle of Change concept in their *1979 Annual Handbook for Group Facilitators.* This five-stage model is based on the Kubler-Ross grief cycle.

Take a look at the graph below and then I'll break it down for you. This will be useful, I promise.

The Emotional Cycle of Change

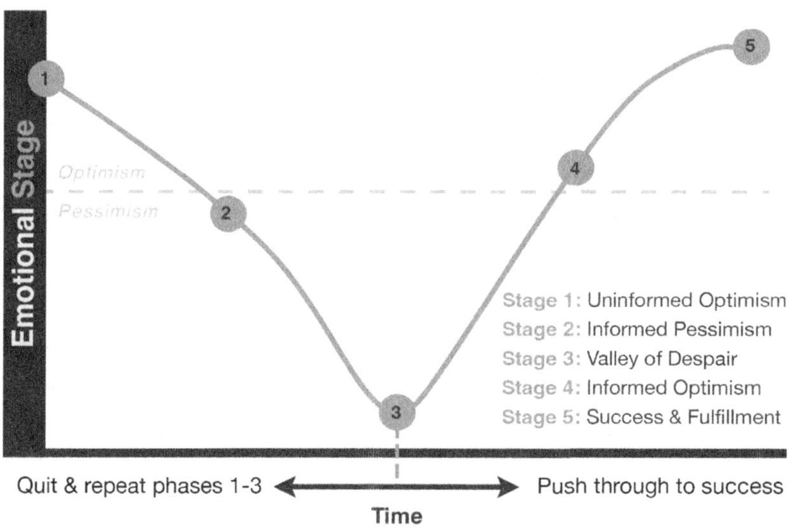

Stage 1: Uninformed Optimism: Take a look at the graph above. "See Stage 1: Uninformed Optimism?" This is the beginning- when the decision you've made to change is exciting. You're thinking about all of the positive possibilities and have not yet considered the challenges ahead. In this stage, you are feeling very optimistic about the future outcome.

Stage 2: Informed Pessimism: As you can see from the graph, this is where reality starts to sink in. You're aware of what it's going to take to make changes, and it may start to *feel* more difficult to reach your desired outcome. At this point, you may be wondering if it's all "worth it," and you may start to find reasons to stop.

Stage 3: Valley of Despair: This is the lowest point in the process to change. It all feels difficult. You aren't able to see the benefits, or the benefits feel out of reach. At this point, you are considering quitting because that feels like the easiest way to end the discomfort you are feeling. At this point, you might think, "Meh, it wasn't THAT bad the way it was before!"

The downside with Stage 3, of course, is two-fold: First, it puts you in danger of quitting, which means you will have given up on something important to you. You will have missed out on a prime opportunity for advancement or self-improvement. Plus, let's be honest, quitting sucks and never feels good! Sure, you might experience some initial relief, but then eventually you feel like a failure. You know you have quit on yourself. That sucks; quit often enough and it can become a habit that lowers your self-respect over time.

And second, even if you don't quit altogether, it means you'll have to start all over again at Stage 1 when you do resume.

So how do you make it through this low point? It's having a really good reason to keep going, a crystal-clear vision of your desired outcome. I'll have more to say on that in a second. First, let's take a look at the final two stages.

Stage 4: Informed Optimism: You are back on track in this stage! You have pushed through the most difficult phase and found your way back to feeling optimistic about the benefits. You are starting to notice that your hard work is paying off and feeling good about what's to come.

Stage 5: Success & Fulfillment: You've made it! You reached your level of success. Everything you've been doing up to this point has paid off, and you realize it's all been worth it. If you have been working on new habits or patterns, they now have become routine.

Getting Past the "I Quit" Point

10 Keys to Success

Most men hit the 'I Quit' point in their health journey because they lack motivation. They may have started with a strong intention, but as time passes and life gets in the way, their enthusiasm wanes.

Let me give you the 10 keys to make sure this doesn't happen to you.

Key No. 1: Get to Your *Deepest* "Why"

The first key to getting past this roadblock is to "rediscover your 'why'."

I know you've probably heard the phrase "find your why" a thousand times before, but here's the thing: Setting goals that don't truly matter to you is like trying to run a race in flip-flops. Sure, you may be able to make it a few steps, but eventually you're going to trip and fall.

Think of your "why" as the anchor that keeps your boat steady in the ocean of change. Just like a boat needs an anchor to stay in one place, your "why" helps keep you focused and motivated during the ups and downs of your health journey. If you lose sight of your "why," it's easy to drift off course and give up.

Jim's Story

Once upon a time, I had a conversation with my client, Jim.

Jim was 51 years old and in the worst shape of his life. He was determined to turn his health around, not just for himself, but for his family as well.

Jim told me that he wanted to lose weight and get in shape because he realized that if he didn't, he would most likely die. (Yes, I know that sounds quite dramatic, but that's really how he felt about it, and with good reason.)

This realization hit him especially hard when he heard about the heart attack and death of his daughter's friend's uncle, who was 10 years younger than Jim and left behind two kids.

When I asked Jim why this was important to him, he replied that he wanted to live a long time for his family. He wanted to be there for them, to support and guide them, and to see his daughter grow up. He also believed that getting in shape would have a positive impact on his professional life, as he would have the energy and patience to be more engaged and there for his employees.

I then asked Jim why now was different from the other times he had tried to make changes. He said he was out of time and that there were no more "laters."

He realized he needed to take action — *now.*

This was the moment.

Fueled by a strong enough "why," Jim was able to overcome any urge to quit and promptly lost 25 pounds. This was the first time he weighed less than 200 pounds in many years. As a result, he was able to wear clothes he hadn't fit into in several years, and to say he felt better would have been a radical understatement. He practically bursted with energy; his increased confidence was obvious to everyone who saw him.

Why am I telling you this story?

It's to show you that everyone has their own defining moment. Sometimes that moment is as big and dramatic as a heart attack ... but just as often, it's something small, maybe even just a glance in the mirror at just the right time, or a quiet inward voice that says, "That's it- I've finally had enough."

Regardless of how it arrives, it always signals the same thing: *Something. Must. Change.*

And it's only when you have *that* type of moment, coupled with a strong enough "why," that makes the pain of staying feel worse than the pain of change.

Only then will you know that you will make it past the "I Quit" point.

I urge you to dig deep to find your own "why" so that you can overcome the "I Quit" point you may end up facing in your own health journey.

I can guarantee you it's worth it!

What to Start with Right Now:

1. Identify and find meaning in your "why." Start with a broad statement of why you want to improve your health. An example could be: "I want to live a long time for my family." (Then get specific: Name your family members, write some sentences explaining exactly WHY you feel this way. Really paint the picture so that you feel it deep in your bones.)

2. Now ask "why" five more times to get to the deeper, more meaningful roots of your motivation. Each time you ask yourself "why," delve deeper into the reasons behind your initial statement.

   Let me show you an example.

Let's say your initial statement is: "I want to have more energy and drop 25 pounds."

That's fine, but it's not enough. That's not enough to generate the feelings you'll need to persevere. So, dig deeper into this initial statement to get to the root of your motivation. Use the following questions:

- **Question:** Why do you want to have more energy and drop 25 pounds?
- **Your Answer Might Be:** "I have very little energy. I stay stressed out. I'm overweight. I hate looking at myself in the mirror. I don't like the father I have become. I don't like the friend I have become."

- **Question:** Why is that reason important to you right now?
- **Your Answer Might Be:** "I'm concerned if I don't start now, then I'm going to let every excuse keep me from doing what is best for my health and my future, and another decade will go by. I can't afford another decade to waste."

- **Question:** Okay. Why is *that* important?
- **Your Answer Might Be:** "I want to be here long term for my wife and my children. I want to be in good shape. I want to be healthy. I want to feel so much better than I feel right now."

- **Question:** Okay, that's great ... But what difference will that REALLY make? Spell it out and make it real.
- **Your Answer Might Be:** "It will mean the world to me. That's the difference in having something to live for versus not even understanding what there is to live for and just going through "the motions" each day."

- **Question:** Okay, so why does *that* even matter?
- **Your Answer Might Be:** "I'm tired of going through the "motions." I want to have "emotion" and LIVE again!"

  Do you see how continually asking yourself, "Okay, so why does THAT matter?" over and over again forces you to go deeper to find the more meaningful reasons?

  This is precisely how you build a rock solid "why" as your motivation. This self-questioning might seem obvious, or a waste of time, but I'm telling you that this is some of the most valuable table setting you can do for yourself. If you skip this process, or go through it superficially, you're just setting yourself up for failure. Keep your deepest "whys" at the forefront of your mind as you work towards your health goals. And when you feel discouraged, return to these "whys" and let them soak in again.

The above example is just one possible way to use the 5 "why" questions. If the questions above don't feel right to you, then phrase them in your own words. The purpose is to dig DEEP to get to the root of your motivations. You may even need to ask "why" *more* than five times. (It's possible you could also need less than five questions, too. Let your gut feeling guide you.)

The goal is to dig deep enough to identify what truly motivates you and keep you pushing past the "I Quit" Point.

Key No. 2: Focus on Actions, Not Outcomes

The second key to getting off the endless rollercoaster of "starting and stopping" is to focus on your actions and not be overly fixated on your outcomes.

Listen, when you're cruising down the road of life toward your goal, you're bound to hit a few speed bumps. But instead of spinning your wheels and getting discouraged by what you can't control, (traffic, weather, etc.), shift your focus to the things you *can* control. That's right, YOU control this car, no one else! The steering wheel is in *your* hands.

Think about it like this: When you're driving somewhere, you can't control the traffic or road conditions. But you *can* control how you navigate, how you handle roadblocks, and how you stay laser-focused on reaching your destination.

Here's another tip: Take small, manageable steps towards your goal, instead of trying to tackle everything at once. To extend the driving analogy further, think about driving from New York to Los Angeles in the dark — you could literally accomplish that simply by keeping your headlights on and taking it 25 yards at a time.

And so, for example, instead of obsessing over losing 25 pounds, focus instead on making healthier food choices at least 80 to 90 percent of the time and working out at least 3 to 4 times a week. Those actions are well within your control.

Instead of throwing in the towel at the first sign of trouble, stay the course, control what you can, and watch your success grow.

What to Start with Right Now:

1. Break your goal down into smaller, actionable steps you can measure. For example, instead of focusing on the goal of losing 25 pounds, you could focus on eating healthier meals at least 80 to 90 percent of the week and getting in 3 to 4 resistance workouts a week, focusing on different muscle groups and using proper form.

2. Focus on the things you can control, not what you can't. This means taking action on the steps you've identified, no matter how small they may seem.

3. Keep track of your progress. Whether it's a journal, a whiteboard, or a tracking app, having a clear picture of what you've accomplished can help you stay motivated and focused on what's important.

4. Celebrate your successes, no matter how small they may be. Achieving your goal is a marathon, not a sprint, so take the time to recognize and appreciate your progress along the way.

Key No. 3: Forgive Yourself If You Screw Up

The third key to help you keep going when you want to call it quits is to get out of the "all-or-nothing thinking" mentality and give yourself a break when you fall short or "screw up."

To illustrate this, I'd like to share the story of my client, James.

James's Story

Tell me if you've ever experienced this before ...

You were striving for something; you were on this incredible winning streak, and then suddenly ... you slipped up.

You instantly felt like a failure, right?

I can relate! And so could James, one of my clients. As a high-powered attorney with a jam-packed schedule full of responsibilities, he was doing all the right things to improve his health and raise his energy levels.

But he had what I call "the false start syndrome."

What do I mean by that?

Well, he'd start dropping weight, his clothes would fit better, but then everything would soon come to a crashing halt.

That was his pattern. But when he joined my Accelerated Method coaching program, he decided this time it would be different.

And for a time, it *was* ...

He hit the ground running just like he did with everything else in his life. He was determined to win. And for the first couple of weeks, that's exactly what he did.

He was on fire. He didn't miss a beat.

In fact, he was following his prescribed routine more faithfully than probably anyone I'd ever seen. He literally wasn't missing a single thing.

And then Week 4 rolled around ...

He went on a business trip for a few days. I'll let James tell the story from here:

"Man, I was on this crazy winning streak, but the second I got out of my routine... I caved. When we went out to restaurants, I just blew it. I overindulged. Then I went back to my hotel room and ate even more. Plus, I missed my workout every day I was gone. I didn't follow any part of my routine, and now I feel like a failure."

On paper, it doesn't sound like the end of the world. But in the moment, it can definitely feel that way.

Have you ever been in a similar situation? Did you ever screw up and think, "Well, I fell off the wagon. *Again.* Why even bother?"

If so, I get it.

I've experienced this, too, as I'm a high performer just like you are.

Once you're on a winning streak, you want to stay on that winning streak. Then one random day sneaks up, slaps you in the face, and throws you off.

Winning streak over. Then the inevitable thoughts pop into your head...

"Well, shoot. I might as well write off the whole thing. At least the rest of the week... Maybe even the rest of the month. Why bother?"

Full disclosure: I've had tons of those thoughts! But I learned something from them.

That kind of all-or-nothing thinking will literally kill long-term progress.

Trust me, I speak from experience.

What's the solution to this "all or nothing" thinking?

Simply focus on the NEXT step. That's it! Sounds super simple, but it *works.*

Let's say you slip with your nutrition for one reason or another. Don't view that as a failure. *Learn from it.*

Let's say you overindulged...

Hey, it happens. The solution is to **simply focus on the next meal.**

In other words, rather than beat yourself up about it, or entertain the idea of quitting, you ask yourself these questions instead:

- *What does breakfast look like?*
- *What does lunch look like?*
- *What does dinner look like?*

Or let's say you missed your morning routine and couldn't get in an early morning quick workout.

Okay, no drama. No big deal.

Simply look at the next part of your day to see where you can still get it in. You could ask yourself:

- *What's my next step of the day — could it fit there?*
- *Let me take a look at my daily calendar for today ... where could I still fit "me" in to make sure I keep progressing?*
- *If not, where could I get creative and approximate at least a portion of what I had intended to do?*

At the end of the day, we're all human. You're going to have ups, you're going to have downs.

And as cool as it would be, you're not the Terminator, sorry.

We're not robots. Focusing on a rigid structure that doesn't allow flexibility and forgiveness isn't the answer. That kind of 'set-in-stone' structure is asking for trouble right off the bat.

So I have a challenge for you.

Next time you find yourself making strides on your goals, but then you slip up unexpectedly, don't sweat it when that "why bother" feeling creeps in, (and it will).

Give yourself a little forgiveness. You're a real-life human balancing a million and one goals, after all. The best thing you can do is gain awareness from those thoughts of doubt.

Be aware that it's okay to slip up. Be willing to focus on the next thing.

Key No. 4: Finish What You Start Despite How It Feels

The fourth key to holding the line and finishing what you started is to **act despite how you "feel."**

Look, there is no such thing as permanent motivation. I'm here to tell you that right now. It's called being human. You will not always feel motivated or inspired to take action.

Think about the last time you were at a business event when you were so pumped that you took notes furiously and put *asterisks* next to all the action items you were going to complete the moment you got back to the office.

And then ... you landed back in reality. Your schedule is still busy as ever, your days inevitably get chaotic. And those action items that were so exciting back at the seminar? Well, suddenly they're now "tabled" for later and have found their way straight into your "Someday" folder for when "the time is right."

You're not always going to feel "in the flow." Motivation comes and goes. You have high days and low days.

And look, I'm right there with you. There are days when I feel like absolute death. Whether it's waking up early to do my morning routine, fitting in my daily workout, or anything related to my physical health and well-being — sometimes I'm just not feeling it. There are days when

I'd rather poke my eyes out with red hot cigars than do The Right Thing.

But guess what? ***That's normal!*** And that's why I'd like you to focus on taking action first rather than waiting for motivation to show up. It doesn't always. But that doesn't matter! It might sound backwards, but motivation will come along if you just take action first.

Listen to my client Andrew's story.

Andrew's Story

Andrew is one of my rockstar clients in my Accelerated Method coaching program. He's a high performer in his 40s, (just like all my clients).

After a long business trip, Andrew got derailed. He wasn't following through on the normal commitments he set for himself.

So I asked him how he was going to end this slump.

His strategy was brilliant and I suggest you take note of it. I'll let Andrew explain it in his own words:

"Today, I'm back in the swing of things," he told me. "Meaning: I'm planning to get back on my bike. But here's the thing — *I know I'm going to feel like absolute shit.* So here's what I do: I tell myself I'm going to give it just 10 minutes and see where it goes from there."

"That's what I do every time I'm in that mindset. I set a timeframe of just 5 to 10 minutes, and I just see how it goes. If I'm not feeling it after that, I call it, no worries."

I love this! Do you see how ingenious this is? Andrew gives himself permission to quit on those days where he's "not feelin' it."

But don't miss the key part here: He doesn't get to quit outright. Instead, he makes himself a grand bargain — he can quit if he wants to, but only after he shows up and makes a very nominal effort of just 10 minutes.

This works because:

a. it's easy to make a very small effort when you know you can quit if you want after just a few minutes; and

b. 9 times out of 10, you end up finishing your entire workout anyway! That's just how it works when you get your blood moving and into the groove of whatever your workout happens to be. *Even after just 10 minutes.*

Trust me, this really works. It's also quite liberating. That's because not every day will be fueled by motivational firepower. That's just not how life operates.

You're not going to feel that way all the time. I don't. And you shouldn't expect that either. Because here's the truth: It's okay to not feel okay.

But if you want to get the results you want, you've got to be willing to move forward despite how you feel. The "10 Minute Bargain" is a nice workaround for that.

So give it a shot: Next time you're not "feelin' it" and you think you're about to call it quits on your goals for good, I encourage you to implement Andrew's counterintuitive strategy: Set a short timer and give yourself permission to "call it" when the timer ends.

Even if you DO quit after 10 minutes, you'll have "won" anyway because you did not give up on yourself. You didn't quit. And I can almost guarantee you that you'll get back to full speed the next day. That's just how it works.

Key No. 5: Calculate the Real Cost of Inaction

The fifth key to getting out of the "I Quit" cycle is to overcome your underlying fears and calculate the real cost of inaction.

As human beings, we're excellent at overestimating the risks of taking action.

We constantly factor in things like:

How much will it cost?

Will it work or not?

How much time and effort will it take?

What will others think?

But what about the risks of NOT taking action?

We're great at justifying and *underplaying* those.

Things like:

...the thousands lost per year in income because the

energy and the focus just isn't there to produce at the highest level possible and get all the important tasks done

...the years of quality time missed with the children and grandkids due to being too tired or worse, (illness or early mortality)

...being the guy who ends up having to take medication the rest of his life

...the wasted hours at work because of a lack of energy and low productivity born of poor habits, (leading to working in the evenings and missing out on quality time with loved ones, too)

...the extra money spent buying "baggier" clothes to hide problem areas like an ever-growing beer gut, rather than fitting back into the sharp, comfortable clothes already hanging in the closet

...the missed opportunities from lacking the extra energy, drive, and confidence that was once there

...strained relationships due to being moody and less understanding

...loss of respect from those we love and lead

OUCH. That's quite a list. (An expensive one at that!)

Think of the irony of someone who's hesitant to try something for fear of failure... but then is already engaging in expensive, risky outcomes simply by not trying at all!

It makes no sense… but I get it, too. It's human nature.

However, once you get clarity on this, you can solve it, for good.

And your first step is to calculate the real cost of inaction rather than bailing on your goals yet again.

What to Start with Right Now:

1. Make a list of all the costs of inaction, including financial, health, personal, and relationship impacts.
2. Reflect on how these costs affect you currently and how they could impact you in the future.
3. Use this list as a motivator to take action towards your goals.
4. Remember that the real cost of inaction is higher than the risk of taking action, and use this to overcome fear of failure.

Key No. 6: Manage Your Expectations

The sixth key to avoiding the quit cycle and staying the course with your goals is to manage your expectations.

We've all been there, brimming with excitement and ready to tackle our goals head-on.

But before we know it, life throws us a curveball, and we find ourselves ready to throw in the towel (again).

Sound familiar?

It's a common scenario and one that often stems from a lack of patience and unrealistic expectations.

You see, when you're filled with excitement and ambition, it's easy to paint a picture in your head of what success will look like. But often that picture is too rosy, too perfect, and too unrealistic.

And when reality doesn't meet your expectations, it can feel like a letdown. Suddenly, the journey to your goals doesn't seem worth it, and quitting seems like the easiest option.

But the truth is, success is rarely a straight line. There will be twists and turns, ups and downs, and moments where it feels like nothing is going right.

Think of it like this: If you want to turn a barge into a speedboat, it's not going to happen overnight. It's going to take patience, perseverance, and a willingness to weather the turbulence along the way.

The same goes for your health goals. You can't expect to go from zero to superhero in a matter of weeks. It takes time, dedication, and effort.

So, how do you avoid the quit cycle and stay motivated towards your goals?

It's simple: **Manage your expectations and give yourself time.**

Think of time as your ally, not your enemy. Give yourself the time you need to achieve your goals, and you'll find that the process becomes much more manageable.

Be honest with yourself about what you can realistically achieve, and then break your goals down into smaller, more achievable milestones.

This way, you'll have a clear roadmap to follow, and you'll be able to celebrate your progress along the way.

So, the next time you find yourself ready to throw in the towel, stop and reassess your expectations. Then, adjust your approach and get back on the road to success, one small step at a time.

Key No. 7: Avoid Shiny Object Syndrome

The seventh key to getting out of the never-ending "stop/start cycle" is to consistently stick to one effective core method, strategy, or routine long enough to see results.

The path to success is often littered with abandoned goals and failed attempts.

Why do so many people fall short of their aspirations?

The answer is simple: lack of consistency.

The reality is, most people are not patient enough to stick with one core strategy long enough to see its true potential.

Instead, they jump from method to method like a hungry goldfish hopping from one shiny object to the next.

But here's the catch — you can't expect to reap the benefits from a strategy if you haven't stuck with it for the long haul. The key is to find what works for you and then stick with it, (even when the going gets tough).

This reminds me of a quote my mentor shared from Shane Parrish, a highly successful entrepreneur and the brains behind one of the world's fastest-growing websites.

Shane said:

> ***"Ninety percent of success can be boiled down to consistently doing the obvious thing for an uncommonly long period of time without convincing yourself that you're smarter than you are."***

Now, this really hit me between the eyes. (Read it again if you have to. It's worth it.)

That's because there were lots of times I found something that worked and was generating all kinds of results.

But then suddenly, *for no good reason,* I would drop the strategy like a hot potato to do something completely different.

My problem was simple: impatience and thinking that a different strategy would produce even bigger results.

Jumping around like this is known as the "shiny object syndrome." And it's a sure recipe for failure.

People who suffer from this constantly say to themselves, "Well, I'll try this thing 'cause it's the latest and greatest fad. I'll see if it works. If it doesn't, I can just jump to the next thing."

No, no, no, no! First of all, never use the word, *"try."* The word "try" implies you're not going to give it your full effort. It's a word that has failure built into it. And it also feeds into shiny object syndrome because it also implies you can just "try" something else.

Stop trying. Just DO. And stick with it long enough to see results.

Otherwise, you'll be saddled with an inability to finish projects, never getting to see the results that truly matter.

Individuals with shiny object syndrome tend to focus on the *novelty* of pursuing a particular strategy rather than on the *strategy itself.*

For example, in the business world, they might fall in love with the idea of developing a new product and begin working on it like there's no tomorrow.

However, they never develop a long-term game plan to make that fuzzy concept gloriously real. They soon move onto something else, only to repeat the same vicious cycle.

If you can't stick to something, you'll find yourself in a never-ending stop/start cycle that will keep you from reaching your goals.

In over 10 years of working with high-performing clients, I've found that the guys who've enjoyed the greatest success are the ones able to stick with their routines, habits, and rituals for an uncommonly long period without constantly jumping ship.

If you want to experience maximum success, find a plan you can stick to.

If it produces results after a reasonable amount of time (and I do mean reasonable), keep doing that thing over and over and over again.

That way, you'll be sure to achieve your dreams.

Don't be a quitter. Be a "stickler." Find your strategy,stick with it, and you'll find success is just around the corner.

Key No. 8: Push Past the Valley of Despair

The eighth key to pushing past the "valley of despair" and reaching ultimate success and fulfillment is to fully commit.

Commitment is the secret ingredient that turns your goals from a fleeting thought into a tangible reality. It's the backbone that supports you through the tough times and helps you overcome the "I quit" point.

Think of commitment to your goals just like a committed relationship.

Just as a successful partnership requires effort, trust, and dedication, so does achieving your goals.

When you make a commitment to a goal, you're investing your time, energy, and resources into something that matters to you. And just like in a committed relationship, it takes more than just an initial spark of interest to make it work — it takes consistent effort and a steadfast determination to see it through.

By committing to your goals, you're making a conscious decision to prioritize what's important to you and to allocate your resources accordingly.

In short, commitment is what sets you apart from the half-hearted dreamers who never make it past the "I quit" point. So, if you're striving to be the best version of yourself, don't be afraid to get serious about your commitment and see it through to the end.

Let me share a quote from one of my mentors:

"

> *"Our outer world reflects our inner commitments. If we want to know what we're really committed to, all we have to do is look at our lives. We are, whether we are aware of it or not, always creating exactly what we're most committed to. The choices we make are always in alignment with our deepest commitments. By examining what we have and what we don't have, we are able to uncover and see what we are truly committed to."*

Key No. 9: Get Some Skin In the Game

The ninth key to bypassing the "I quit" lane and getting on the fast-track to success is to bet on yourself and put some skin in the game.

If you're serious about achieving your goals, consider that you can't just sit on the sidelines and hope for the best. You have to get in the game, and that means putting some skin in it.

Think about it this way: Have you ever gotten something for free and then not valued it as much as if you had paid for it? We all have- it's human nature. If something's free, we often assume it can't be very good. Free isn't always the best option.

I learned this the hard way. I used to think that getting free information was the best way to grow and achieve success. But I soon learned that "free" was quite expensive. When I didn't have anything invested in my own personal growth, I didn't take it seriously. I didn't fully commit to the process, and as a result, my results were lackluster.

It wasn't until I started betting on myself and putting some real skin in the game that I began to see exponential growth in my life.

You see, when you invest your hard-earned money into something, you're more likely to pay attention, take it seriously, and work harder to make it a success.

So, don't be afraid to bet on yourself and put some real skin in the game. Your success is worth the investment.

Key No. 10: Accountability

Accountability is the key ingredient to turning your "I quit" attitude into an "I got this!" mindset.

Having someone hold you accountable to a higher

standard will do wonders to help you hit your goals consistently, even on days when quitting seems like the easiest option.

So why is accountability crucial for success? Simply put, we are more likely to stick to our commitments when we have someone checking in on us and reminding us of why we started in the first place. Plus, it's a lot harder to back out of a promise you made to someone else, rather than just yourself.

Accountability is like having a personal sherpa for your life goals. Just as a sherpa guides a mountaineer to the summit, your accountability partner provides direction, support, and encouragement as you navigate the ups and downs of your journey.

Let's face it, you have many responsibilities and competing priorities, but with an accountability partner by your side, you have a trusted guide who helps you stay focused, overcome obstacles, and reach new heights. Whether you're setting out on a personal or professional journey, your accountability partner is there to offer encouragement, offer advice, and help you reach the top.

I recommend finding someone outside of your immediate family or friend group who will level with you and tell you what you *need* to hear, (rather than just what you *want* to hear), so that you can push past your obstacles and reach your desired outcome.

Personally, I have always thrived off having a coach or a mentor in my corner to point out my blind spots.

They have held me accountable and helped me get out of my own way. I've condensed the amount of time it would have normally taken for me to hit goals on my own because I was held to a higher standard.

You reach your desired outcomes sooner when you are held accountable.

This is why my team and I hold every client accountable in a way that inspires them to take action.

Our high-impact accountability and personal attention are two main reasons my clients see better results in 12 weeks than most stand-alone students see in 12 months.

It is crucial to have someone who understands your current situation and doesn't come down on you if you mess up, but also doesn't default to telling you what you want to hear all of the time. You want someone who can easily walk the line of being your collaborator and your coach. You need this person to level with you and be in your corner always.

I would love to show you how to go from sick and tired to "back on fire" and become the man you want to be.

I invite you to get in contact with me or a member of my team by visiting: *https://www.acceleratedmethod.com/call*

We can customize your approach and tailor each step of this process to your specific needs.

Key Chapter Takeaways

- Understand that change can be difficult and that anything new can feel risky. Be aware that your mind (and ego) wants to play it safe. Use the following 10 keys to combat that reality, lest you get derailed in reaching your goals:
- Get to your deepest "why."
- Focus on actions, not outcomes.
- Give yourself a break if you screw up!
- Become a "finisher" even if it feels uncomfortable.
- Calculate the real (and usually hidden) cost of inaction.
- Manage your expectations.
- Avoid Shiny Object Syndrome.
- Push past the Valley of Despair.
- Get some skin in the game!
- Get some accountability in order to stay on track.

CASE STUDY

Jim C., Texas, VP of Operations

Breaking Bad Habits: Jim's Success Story

"I didn't have much energy. I was always buying new clothes because the other ones didn't fit anymore. Not eating good. Not drinking any water. My liquid intake on a daily basis was Diet Coke or beer.

I'd get home from work and just sit around, watch TV, and cook dinner, but I wasn't excited or energetic and just kind of wanted to be in my own little world. Since joining, life's gotten better. A lot more focused. Both at work and at home. One of the benefits is the people around you see what you're doing and want to get involved. My daughter, she's pleased with the progress. My wife is really pleased with the progress. I've lost about 25 pounds, I'm below 200 pounds for the first time and I went down three notches on a belt. I've been able to wear clothes I haven't worn in probably seven or eight years. I feel 100 times better, with more energy. And I'm more confident with the way I look."

— Jim C., Texas, VP of Operations

CHAPTER 12

The Secret to Achieving Your Goals (That No One Tells You About)

How is it that two people can have the exact same plan, tools, routines, and resources… as well as the exact same daily stresses, time constraints, commitments, and obligations to fulfill…

And yet, one of them succeeds, and the other can't follow through on their goals?

The answer lies in their *mindset.*

I know you've heard the term "mindset" a bunch of times, and you might think you know what it means. But there are some critical aspects as it specifically relates to regaining your edge that need to be said.

Let's start with this: Your mindset is composed of your own personal beliefs and assumptions that are so powerful, your behavior will literally conform to them.

As a result, **new results require new behaviors… and new behaviors require new beliefs and assumptions.**

Please don't let those previous two paragraphs slide by! There's more there than you might think.

Here's another sentence you might want to read twice before moving on:

By believing the same things you've always believed in, your behavior might change for a few days or a few weeks, *but before you know it you're back down the rabbit hole, (and stuck in the same situation), right back where you started.*

Any time someone initiates a change in their life there are two phases we need to think about:

1. Their current reality, (where they are now).
2. Their ideal reality, (where they want to go).

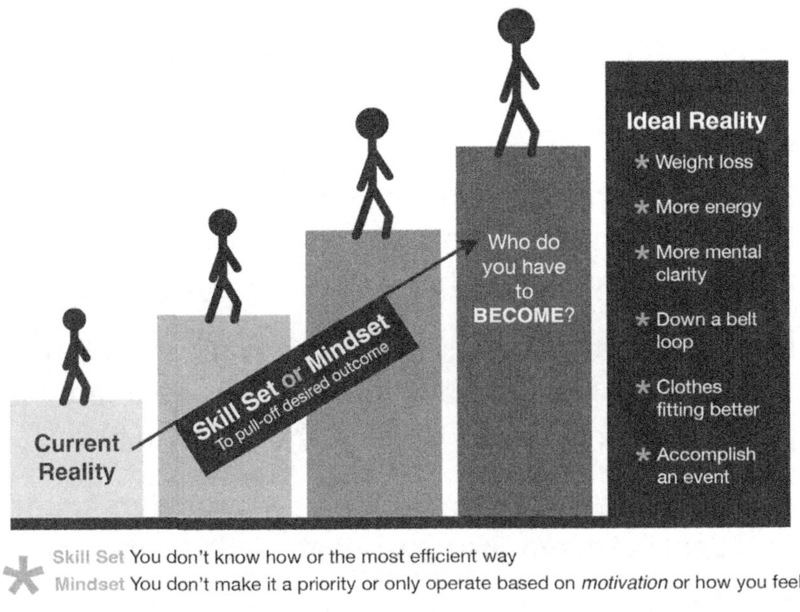

The current reality may be:

> "I'm tired of being tired and drained."
>
> "I'm not proud of the guy staring back at me in the mirror."
>
> "I don't like how my clothes are fitting."
>
> "I don't like being short and snappy with those closest to me."
>
> "I'm fed up with getting rattled easily and getting constantly derailed from my goals."

And the ideal reality may be:

> "I'm at my perfect weight."
>
> "I have tons of energy."
>
> "I have mental clarity all day long."
>
> "My clothes fit way better (and look better) on me again."
>
> "I'm much more patient and understanding with those around me."
>
> "I'm accomplishing my goals more quickly and easily."

Don't worry if your particular goals differ from the ones above. That's just one before-and-after scenario (but a common one for guys I work with). The point is, whatever *your* goals are, there exists a new and improved reality that you're moving toward. It's your dream outcome.

But what you may not realize is that your current reality is based just as much on ***who you ARE*** as ***what you DO.***

Again, you might have to let that sink in to fully get it.

Here's another way to put it: Your current situation isn't just a result of all your behaviors, actions, and choices. It's also *how you see yourself, your identity at its core.*

If you're wondering why your current behavior clashes with your ideal reality, it's because the two cannot exist in the same space.

So how do we get to that ideal reality?

It's not just about having the right tools, skill sets, and systems in place to get to where you want to go- *it's also about* ***who you have to become*** *to accomplish that goal.*

The new person who shows up differently and makes different decisions. The new person who makes themselves a priority.

You have to ***become*** this new person to pull off your ideal reality.

However, based on my experience, there are two crucial factors that might be standing in your way:

First, you might not know exactly HOW to do this or what "becoming that person" even means in the first place! (If so, no worries, keep reading, I've got you covered.)

Second, you actually DO know what to do … but you don't do it! Or you can't bring yourself to do it.

This second problem is thornier, more insidious. Why? Because failing to take action when you know better indicates some sort of mental paradigm holding you back. I'm not just talking about preconceived notions, (although you may have plenty of those, too). I'm talking about a frame of mind that's practically baked into your very being — so much so that it's become who you are.

My ear has become attuned to certain "giveaway" phrases that tell me a high performer needs help in closing this type of "identity gap" before they can enact real change in their life.

For example, tell me if even one of these sounds familiar:

> *"I don't have the time or energy to figure all this out."*
>
> *"I don't even know where to start in 'becoming' this new person you're talking about."*
>
> *"This is too selfish for me to even consider."*
>
> *"Doesn't matter what I do, it's never good enough anyway."*
>
> *"Honestly, I'd rather just let it go than to try and fail."*
>
> *"I'm just not cut out to follow through on something like this."*
>
> *"Well, whatever. It is what it is."*
>
> *"Look, this is just what happens after you turn 40."*
>
> *"Sometimes you simply have to accept this is how it is."*
>
> *"Why bother, what's the point?"*

Can you just *hear* the self-defeating frame of mind at work here?

Don't feel bad if any of these sound like you. This is very common and quite natural — and, thankfully, reversible!

I'll say it again: The No. 1 problem I see among my clients trying to level up and get results that last is that they either don't know what to do, or they do know what to do but just don't do it.

They have some form of "unconscious break" that holds them back.

I call this break the **Identity Dilemma.**

The Identity Dilemma

There is a gap between who you are now and who you need to become.

From what I've seen with my clients, most people allow themselves to go on autopilot. They unconsciously make choices that, in so many words, translate to: "This is who I am. This is how it is."

"*Well, Logan, it is what it is…*" is something I hear a lot.

But here's the thing — that's defeatist. Whether you know it or not, you actually *have* more control than that. Your current situation doesn't *have* to be inevitable.

You do that most effectively by changing your identity. When you change your identity, improving your life can become almost effortless rather than trying to push a huge boulder uphill.

Let's back up a bit, so that I can explain. This is important.

Your identity is created from past experiences. Your past experiences create your current stories, beliefs, habits, patterns, behaviors, and results.

Let me tell you about a high-performing attorney in my program named Benjamin.

By the time Benjamin joined the Accelerated Method program, he had already tried several programs and methods, all to no avail. He saw some minor changes, but they never lasted.

After he got tremendous results with my program, I asked him what made it different from the others.

He told me, "Aside from gaining the energy and dropping the weight, what made this different was the mental aspect. I had no clue that I could have anything to do with me getting results! Seems silly for me to admit that, but I just didn't realize the power of it."

This is all too common in the men I work with.

Do you want to know why so many otherwise intelligent men operate at a high-performing level at work but fail miserably when it comes to their health?

It's not because they're busy. ***It's because they're missing that crucial mental component!***

Too many people believe that the programs, diets, and pills are the ones doing the work. That's why, when reality hits, they crumble.

Programs don't fail people. People fail the programs.

And a chronic lack of success isn't about some moral failing, mind you. It's because the person's inner paradigm hasn't changed. It's like they haven't updated their internal software since Windows 95, so no wonder they're crashing all the time.

That's a joke, but the analogy holds. That's why, even with the best of intentions, some guys crumble at the first sign of weakness. All it takes is a single monkey wrench thrown into their week and pretty soon they're calling it quits.

It's because **they haven't changed *on the inside.***

Look, there are a lot of effective systems out there, including some with great coaches and proven methods.

But they are only tools. They don't make the difference, ***you do***. The person you mentally see yourself as. If you want change to stick, you need to see yourself as someone who is invested in your health.

You need to see yourself as:

- A guy who is in great shape regardless of his age.
- A guy who has energy.
- A guy who looks, feels, and performs his best.

These aren't just hopeful wishes. These need to become your unshakeable identity.

This mindset shift will ultimately place you in a position of power, which will let you pursue, achieve, and sustain your results in a permanent way.

What about motivation? What *about* it! Here's the problem: *Motivation is fleeting*. As I tell my clients, motivation is more fickle than the weather. And can I let you in on a secret? I myself don't always feel like waking up at a decent time to put myself and my health first!

It's true ...

- I don't always want to wake up early to do my morning routine.
- I don't always feel like sticking to my diet and nutrition.
- I don't always feel like getting to bed at a certain time.
- I don't always feel like doing the things that will increase my energy levels.
- I don't always feel motivated to do the things that I know will be beneficial to my overall health and wellness.

It's true. I'm only human. And so are you.

But here's what separates me from someone who hasn't done this crucial, inner identity work: I know deep down I'm the kind of person who mostly sticks to the activities and routines that keep me physically fit and mentally sharp.

Notice I said "mostly." I don't always. But I always get back on track very quickly. Why? It's because being that fit, sharp guy is who I am.

Whenever counter-productive feelings come up I ask myself, "Who am I being today? Who do I want to be?"

I'll say it again: **You cannot outperform your own self-image.**

Even if you have the greatest plan of action backed by a world-renowned program, you might get results, but they will be short-lived, if you have not changed your self-image to match the outer person you want to be.

It's not what you have to do but *who you need to become in the process.*

This is why having the necessary tools and strategies to master the mental game is essential for lasting results.

The process starts with awareness. You assess where you are now and then take steps to change whatever mindset patterns are not serving you well.

You are in control. You are the master of your conscious self.

By altering awareness, we can make this shift.

Now that you understand how much your identity affects your life outcomes, you're probably wondering exactly HOW to create a new and more positive identity that reflects who you truly want to be. Below is a step-by-step guide to help you get started.

What to Start with Right Now:

I invite you to take some time to reflect and answer the questions below both openly and honestly.

(Important note before you begin: The identity examples below may differ from your own specific situation, but just know that you can use the same steps to create your own new identity and ultimately achieve any goal you want. In other words, it's the process that's important here. Take it to heart and put this exercise to good use for yourself!)

1. **Begin with self-reflection:**

   - What are my values and beliefs? Example: I value health, wellness, and vitality. I believe that I can regain my energy and strength.

   - What are my strengths and weaknesses? Example: I'm good at setting goals and following through, but I struggle with sticking to a routine.

   - What do I enjoy doing? Example: I enjoy hiking, playing basketball, and cooking healthy meals.

   - What are my goals in life? Example: My goal is to regain my energy, strength, and fitness so that I can enjoy an active lifestyle with my family and friends.

   - What type of person do I want to become?

Example: I want to become a fit, healthy, and energetic person who can keep up with my family and enjoy outdoor activities.

2. **Identify the beliefs currently holding you back:**

   - What beliefs do I have about myself that are holding me back? Example: I'm too old to get in shape. I don't have time to exercise.

   - What beliefs do I have about the world that are holding me back? Example: It's too hard to eat healthy.

   - Where did these beliefs come from? Example: These beliefs come from years of neglecting my health and fitness and from societal messages about aging and health.

   - Are these beliefs true, or are they just self-imposed beliefs? Example: These beliefs are self-imposed. Age is just a number;I have what it takes to eat healthier, and there are many time-efficient and accessible ways to improve my health and fitness.

3. **Rewrite your story:**

   - What story am I currently telling myself? Example: I'm too old and tired to get in shape. I don't have time to exercise or eat healthy.

   - What story do I want to tell myself? Example: I am capable of regaining my energy, strength, and fitness. I have the time and resources to make healthy choices and prioritize my wellness.

- How can I change my narrative to align with my ideal reality? Example: I can focus on the positive benefits of exercise and healthy eating such as increased energy and stamina. I can also prioritize my self-care and make time for exercise and meal planning.

4. **Create a new identity statement:**

   - Example: "I am an energized, strong, and fit person who prioritizes my health and wellness. I have the energy and stamina to enjoy an active lifestyle with my family and friends."

5. **Act as if:**

   - How would the person I want to become behave in this situation? Example: The person I want to become would prioritize exercise and healthy eating, even when it's difficult or inconvenient.

   - What choices would they make? Example: They would choose healthy foods and make time for regular exercise.

   - What habits would they have? Example: They would have a consistent exercise routine and prioritize sleep and stress management.

6. **Adjust your language to support your new identity:**

- The language we use can have a significant impact on our thoughts, feelings, and actions. Use language that supports your new identity and reinforces positive beliefs about yourself.

  For example, instead of saying, "I can't do this," say "I am capable of figuring this out." Or instead of saying, "I'm too old for this" when faced with a physical challenge, you can shift your language to say, "I may be older, but I am still capable of being energized, strong, and fit." This change in language reinforces positive beliefs about your abilities and supports your new identity as an energized, strong, and fit person.

7. **Track your progress:**

   - Keep track of your progress by recording your exercise and meals in a journal or app. Celebrate small wins such as completing a workout or making a healthy meal choice.

Two final notes about the above exercise and questions:

First, don't dismiss how powerful these are. These questions are not just for daydreaming. This is literally how you can reprogram your mind to become a better you.

Second, work with them *repeatedly*. Your new identity will not happen overnight, and repetition is how you implant these new beliefs into your very being. Stick with them and make them part of your routine.

As you approach the end of this chapter, it's time to reflect on a key idea that can help you achieve your goals:

If you want to change what you see, you must change how you see things.

Think of it like looking through a pair of binoculars — if you're not focused on the right thing, you might miss something important.

By adjusting your focus and gaining a new perspective, you can see things in a whole new light.

As you consider the insights and ideas presented in this chapter, take some time to think about how you can shift your mindset to achieve greater success. It's easy to get stuck in old ways of thinking and limit yourself with self-imposed beliefs, but by embracing new perspectives, you can open up new opportunities and achieve your goals more easily.

Finally, as you move forward, remember that changing your mindset can change your world.

Keep an open mind, be willing to let go of old beliefs, and stay focused on what truly matters.

With the right mindset and a fresh perspective, there's no limit to what you can achieve.

Key Chapter Takeaways

- Mindset is the reason two guys can have access to the same plan, tools, routines, and resources... but get very different results. Mindset is the difference-maker between success and failure.
- New results require new behaviors. And new behaviors require new beliefs and assumptions.
- There is a gap between your current reality and your ideal reality. This gap is keeping you from hitting your goals.
- An Identity Dilemma can keep you stuck from getting to your ideal reality.
- Your current reality is based just as much on who you ARE as what you DO.
- Cultivate a new self view using the questions in this chapter to bridge the Identity Gap.

CASE STUDY

Chris Y., Texas, High-Level Executive

"I was probably operating at 40 percent to 50 percent energy levels. Now I'm in the 90 percent range with still more room to push myself to the next level."

"I don't wake up tired anymore. I wake up ready to go and it's hard to even put a description around how I feel now. Before this I would tell you I was probably operating at 40 percent to 50 percent energy levels. Now I'm in the 90 percent range with still more room to push myself to the next level. My productivity is intertwined with energy. So my productivity and focus are through the roof.

I mean, I'm getting stuff done quicker, better, faster and being able to get more strategic in my relationships, and you know where I'd get knuckled down in projects and meetings before, I don't worry about that now. I get through what I have to get through and it's allowed me that time back to start working more strategically around relationships and partnerships in our corporations."

—Chris Y., Texas, High-Level Executive

CHAPTER 13

Launch to Victory: Three Essential Steps to Your First Win

We've covered a lot of ground so far: dialing in your health and nutrition, maximizing your energy levels, correcting hormonal imbalances, fixing your sleep, creating your ideal morning routine, and implementing key strategies to keep you on track, and more.

This book was carefully constructed to make all this happen for you in the fastest, most efficient manner possible. It's my sincere hope you take everything in this book and don't make it just something that's interesting to read … but something you put into actual practice.

However, before you go any further, I'd like to share three more elements to this system you need to understand in order to succeed and become truly unstoppable again.

I've assembled these key elements into three important steps:

Step #1 - Set Agreements

Imagine you decide enough is enough, and it's finally time to get your health in order, regain your energy, and get in the best shape of your adult life.

(Fantastic! That's why I wrote this book in the first place.)

And let's say you've set a goal to work out and move three to four times a week, eat healthier, and get to bed at a decent hour to improve your sleep. You're feeling motivated and ready to make it happen.

But let's say you soon realize that the people closest to you don't share the same goals (let alone your renewed enthusiasm). Your significant other is perfectly content with ordering takeout every night, and your friends constantly invite you out to happy hour where they pressure you to drink and indulge in unhealthy foods.

Let's get real. Without agreements in place, it's going to be a tough, uphill battle.

You can't blame *them*, of course. They're free to live their own lives, just as you are.

But you're on a mission. For good reason. This is your *life* we're talking about here! And while it would be unfair to ask your significant other or friends to hop aboard the same self-improvement train you're now on, it's also true that you can expect to face conflicting wants and desires from the people you love and care about. Making it easy to give into peer pressure and temptations.

If you don't take the time to put agreements in place with

those closest to you, it will feel like you're trying to run a marathon with a ball and chain around your ankle. The friction will make it nearly impossible for you to achieve your goals.

On the other hand, if you have agreements in place with those closest to you, things will be much smoother. Your significant other could agree to help you cook healthier meals, for example, and your friends could understand and support your decision to call it early for the night instead of going to happy hour. With their support, you'll find that it's much easier to stick to your goals and make progress.

It's like having a team of coaches pushing you toward the finish line. Sure, it will still take effort on your part, but you'll find that you're able to achieve your goals much faster and with much less friction.

What to Start with Right Now

1. **Identify your goals.** Clearly define what it is you want to achieve and the steps you need to take to get there. Make sure they are specific and measurable.

2. **Communicate your goals.** Share your goals with the people closest to you, including family, friends, and colleagues. Let them know why these goals are important to you and how they can support you.

3. **Set agreements.** Work with the people in your life to establish agreements on how you will support each other in achieving your goals. This may include things like agreeing to specific times for working

out, creating healthy meals together, or setting boundaries around work and personal time. It's up to you how specific and formal you want to make these agreements. Do what's comfortable for you. And remember to keep the lines of communication open, be flexible and willing to adjust as needed.

Step #2 - Stick to Your Schedule & Your Non-Negotiables

Not too long ago, I flew out to Vegas to work with an awesome client of mine for a private VIP day. (This is something I offer some of my 1-on-1 clients.) And one of the topics he brought up was how easy it can be to backslide when life gets in the way.

He said, "Logan, I just get rattled sometimes. And it's not even related to emergency situations. Something from the work front that I wasn't expecting or something on the family front pops up suddenly, and it puts me in reactionary mode. Everything I intended to do that week gets put on the backburner."

This is something a lot of my clients deal with.

If you've experienced this, I get it. I have a very powerful way to overcome this. If you ever find yourself getting rattled from the week, and all your intentions of taking care of yourself fall by the wayside, I suggest you use something I call, "The Sunday Strategy."

The Sunday Strategy

First of all, you should know this is not limited to only Sundays! (It just so happens to be a catchy name, so I went with that.) But really, this strategy is to be used any time before the beginning of your week.

Here's how it works: You sit down in a nice, quiet spot and make sure you have a good game plan for the upcoming week. Now, you probably already have standing meetings, along with other things that can't be moved. You also probably have a lot of people who want your attention.

That's fine. Keep those penciled in. But relax and take at least an hour to really slow down before the next week starts to create a solid game plan for yourself. Below are some things you can either journal about, write into your calendar, or put onto your to-do list. (All three are valid ways to execute the Sunday Strategy; just find a way that works for you.)

You'll want to write about:

- Your top goals for your business for the upcoming week.
- The two or three absolute highest priorities for the week.
- Your client/work obligations.
- Specific times you plan to get workouts in.
- Your planned bedtimes on certain days.
- Family events and obligations.

- Personal goals.
- Anything else that comes to mind.

Write it all out until you feel there's nothing more to add. *Whew* — Doing this alone will give you a sense of relief! It will clear your head- and you will head into the new week without nagging thoughts chasing your sleep every night.

Whether you document all this in your planner, calendar, a notepad you keep on your desk, or a certain app on your phone, you'll be mitigating the chaos that comes your way throughout the week. It's also an insurance policy that protects your all-important non-negotiables.

This is important, so let's get into this a bit.

Building Around Your Non-negotiables

I'd like to clarify what I mean by non-negotiables. As the name implies, non-negotiables are the things you refuse to negotiate on.

These are elements that absolutely align with your goals, principles, and values.

Not only will they dictate what you will and won't accept from others, but they will also dictate what you will and won't accept *from yourself.*

Non-negotiables are promises you keep to yourself and those you love and lead. They are unique to your situation, and only you can determine what they are and how to manage them. When you create non-negotiables in your life, your focus will not waiver.

Here's how to create non-negotiables that serve you:

1. **Get clear.** Create clarity on what your non-negotiables are. Write them down and ensure you're clear on what you refuse to budge on.

2. **Align Yourself.** Make sure each of your non-negotiables are in alignment with your goals and what you deem as MOST important for you to succeed.

3. **Communicate.** It's one thing to determine your non-negotiables, but it's another to actually live by them. Make sure to communicate with those you spend most time with, such as your family, team at work, or friends. Letting other people know what is important to you, and why, will help set a frame around your standards and will allow others to support you and help you stay on track.

Let me share a few examples of non-negotiables my clients commonly use:

- Getting in your morning routine (no email, no work, no messages, no social media, no media/ news ... not until you get YOU in first)
- Being in bed by 10 p.m.
- A monthly massage
- Scheduling some kind of movement (exercise) at least three to four times a week

- Shutting off completely from work by 8 p.m.
- Staying on point with nutrition at least 80 percent to 90 percent throughout the week (including making sure you have certain foods "waiting on deck" that allow you to stay on track)
- Having a 24-hour "Day of Space Away from Work" (no email, no cell phone, no social media ... just time to do things that rejuvenate and recharge you)
- Scheduling weekly date nights with your significant other

Will there be other things flying at you during the week? Of course! That's life. But at least you'll be in control with a solid game plan. No longer will you feel out of control, flying by the seat of your pants in constant "reaction mode."

What to Start with Right Now:

1. Implement the "Sunday Strategy" by taking an hour before the start of your week to create a solid game plan for yourself.

2. Determine your non-negotiables, which are the things you refuse to negotiate on that align with your goals, principles, and values.

3. Create your own list of non-negotiables such as: getting in your morning routine, being in bed by 10 p.m., scheduling movement, shutting off from work, staying on point with nutrition, having a "day of space" away from work, scheduling date nights with

your significant other, or anything else that aligns with your personal and professional goals.

Step #3- Build Structure by Creating Winning Environments

I can't tell you how many times I've heard, "Man, I just feel like I lack willpower."

Here's the thing: **Any plan that requires you to muster loads of willpower usually only works for a very short time frame.**

Trust me, I've realized that from my own experience too. Willpower doesn't work for lasting results.

Willpower doesn't work for sustainability. Mere willpower alone always loses eventually.

I'm not interested in short-term results, and neither should you be. It's all about the long term, isn't it? We all want sustainable energy and results for the next decade and beyond.

So the question becomes: If willpower doesn't work for building long-term success, what does?

Structure

We need to build structure, plans, and habits that are in alignment with our non-negotiables to get us to where we want to go, so we're no longer at the mercy of the winds blowing us every which way.

Without structure, there is no order.

And without order, there's pure chaos.

But with the right structure in place — while still allowing for spontaneity — you'll have the freedom to experience **consistent, predictable, and sustainable results.**

You'll be able to say "no" to distractions and the things that just get in your way, without missing out on opportunities to still have fun and discover new things.

You'll be able to clear the fog, put together a roadmap for where you want to go, and then actually *get* there.

You'll be more focused and more confident in yourself.

You'll see your energy levels go up and the numbers on your bathroom scale go down.

Your "new normal" will be spending time on your favorite hobbies after work or taking your wife for fun nights out, rather than falling asleep on the couch as soon as you've made it through the front door.

With the right structure in your life, all those things you've dreamed of achieving will not only be possible – they'll be *inevitable* because you're now charting your own course instead of just letting life "happen."

One of the best ways to build structure is to **create winning environments.**

Let's face it, every day we're bombarded with tons of choices, (more than you probably realize).

For instance, even seemingly mindless, routine decisions, while not overbearing, DO tax your willpower. This is why people like Steve Jobs, (black shirt and blue jeans), and Mark Zuckerberg, (gray T-shirt), always wore/wear the same thing every day. It was just one less decision for them to make. They understood the freedom that comes with freeing up your mind for more important things.

But of course, it's the more tempting choices that truly test the strength of your willpower and decision making. I'm talking about the ones we try to resist, or put off, which is why they can creep up on us in our weakest moments when we least expect it — or when it's too late to make a smart decision. This too often results in that big slice of double chocolate bundt cake you didn't really need, the extra cocktail that's going to interfere with your sleep tonight, and the tapping of the snooze alarm you're going to regret in the morning.

It's in those moments you weren't able to take measure of those temptations. It was too late. And then you unnecessarily beat yourself up for "not wanting it bad enough."

Which misses the point and is unfair, to boot. Why?

Because these temptations can mostly be prevented by managing your environmental cues ahead of time!

Environmental cues are the things in our surroundings that trigger certain thoughts and desires, causing us to behave in certain ways.

Your decisions are largely influenced by what surrounds you.

For example:

- Your work is too far away from your desk, causing you to procrastinate on getting started.
- The plates you use for dinner have a wide area, so you tend to fill them up with more food than you need.
- Your fridge is filled with tons of crap food, so even if you do have "healthy" options, after a long day of work when you're looking to decompress, you're much more likely to grab the crap food over the good stuff.

Even if you set out to complete a goal with the best of intentions, it's no use if your environment works against you.

Picture yourself on a journey to reach a mountain summit. Your environment is the trail you take to get there. If the trail is well-groomed and free of obstacles, you'll reach the top with ease. However, if the trail is full of detours and distractions, you'll end up losing focus and making poor decisions.

This is why creating winning environments is crucial to reaching your goals. It sets you up for success by making it easy to make the right choices.

Creating structure starts with manipulating your environment to work in your favor. It's like creating a well-defined path to the top of that mountain with markers and signs pointing you toward your goal.

Simply put, if you want to change your behavior and reach your goals, start by changing your environment. Make the path to success easy and clear, and you'll find yourself climbing to new heights in no time.

What to Start with Right Now:

1. **Evaluate your current environment:** Take a look at your surroundings and assess what environmental cues are triggering you to make certain choices. This can include physical cues such as your work setup, the food in your pantry, or the objects in your home, or digital cues like the websites you visit or the apps you use.

2. **Adjust your environment:** Make changes to your surroundings to create a more supportive environment for your goals. This can include physical changes like rearranging your kitchen to make healthy food options more accessible, rearranging furniture to create a designated exercise area, or decluttering your workspace or home to reduce stress.

3. **Add supportive cues:** Add environmental cues that will trigger positive thoughts and actions to help you reach your goals. This can include keeping your goals top of mind by printing them out or putting them as the background of your mobile device,

keeping healthy snacks within reach, or creating a relaxing space to unwind at the end of the day.

4. **Monitor your progress:** Regularly assess your behavior and how your environment is affecting it. If you find that certain cues are no longer helpful or that you need additional support, make the necessary adjustments.

Examples of Environment Changes To Consider:

- For a goal of staying fit, clear your pantry of junk food and stock it with healthy options so that meal prep becomes easy.

  Note: If you find yourself pressed for time, consider delegating your nutrition by ordering a "right to your door" food option, (i.e. online meal prep service/ local meal prep service).

  Keep healthy snacks on deck like low carb protein bars, almonds, and beef sticks that you can take with you on the go. Have a big water bottle near you at all times to remind you to stay hydrated.

- For a goal of increasing physical activity, create a designated exercise area in your home with a mat or weights. Keep your workout gear within reach, lay out your workout clothes the night before, and schedule time for physical activity in your morning routine.

- For a goal of being productive, create a designated workspace with limited distractions. Turn off notifications on your phone, use a productivity tool such as a time tracker, and keep your workspace organized.

- For a goal of reducing stress, create a relaxing environment with calming cues such as soft lighting, and a comfortable reading chair. Consider removing any sources of stress in your home such as a cluttered living room or a TV in your bedroom.

Creating an environment that not only makes you feel good, but also serves your goals by anticipating — and *preventing* — temptations ahead of time, is one of the things I specialize in when working with my private clients. It's a form of productivity insurance- it's like having an invisible bodyguard making sure your highest aspirations are safe from sneak attacks. And you'd be surprised at all the hidden "landmines" in your home and elsewhere that may not have occurred to you! The best part is, the fixes for them are super simple and effective. Let me tell you, when you remove these with a certain intelligence and creativity, you'll stay on track without even thinking about it. If you're interested in hearing more about how we do this for our highest performing clients, then please go to: *https://www.acceleratedmethod.com/call* to book a call with me or one of my team members for more details.

Key Chapter Takeaways

- Use these three steps to ensure your success:

    1. Create non-negotiables by creating clarity, aligning yourself with your goals, and communicating with those around you.

    2. Set agreements with those whom you spend a majority of your time with.

    3. Create winning environments by making sure you remove anything in your environment that acts against you as you set out to win.

CASE STUDY

Elliott S., South Carolina, High-Level Executive

"I knew something was wrong, but I didn't know how wrong it was."

"Looking back on it, I was miserable, and I didn't know it.

I weighed 247 pounds when I started, and today, I weigh 210 pounds.

When you're in survival mode and you're trying to help everybody but yourself, you don't take care of yourself. I kept having very convenient excuses. "I don't have time" was an excuse that always crept in.

When you've got all these other things and responsibilities going on, you almost feel selfish not attending to those first. If you try to put yourself first, sometimes you feel selfish.

I'll never forget the tagline, "The Program for the Busy Man." And I said, "That's me, but that can't be right." But there was just something about Logan. The way he carried himself, the way he talked, I could tell he believed in what he was talking about. It was that moment the lightbulb turned on. I thought, "I don't have an excuse anymore. If what Logan is putting in front of me is real, then I don't have an excuse."

He pushes us to the edge of what he knows we can do. But I've never left feeling hurt. It's about feeling good. Feeling right. Being able to believe in the things I didn't think I could necessarily do. Being able to do things that I never thought I could do before has bred that confidence in all aspects of my life.

When you feel bad for a long time, you don't realize it until you feel good. And once you feel good, you appreciate the things around you.

A lot of people in my life and in my family die at a pretty early age. I used to accept that as a fact. I don't accept it anymore."

— Elliott S., South Carolina, High-Level Executive

CHAPTER 14

Reigniting the Fire Within: A 7-Day Plan to Transform You from 'Sick and Tired' to 'Back on Fire'

Well, well, well — Congratulations! You've made it this far and that tells me two things:

Number one, you're someone who *follows through* and is interested in *getting real results*, rather than just someone who dreams about them.

And number two, it tells me that you're ready to ditch the "sick and tired" blues and ignite that "back on fire" spark.

Great! I never get tired of meeting guys who reach the point of being "sick and tired of being sick and tired" because it's precisely at *that* point that I know they're ready to make a serious change.

Now, I gave a lot of thought as to how I wanted to end this book. And since I'm all about helping you feel better immediately, I decided to put together a 7-day plan that's as simple as pie, but packs a punch. So, dust off that pen, find a blank page in your notebook, and let's get started! It's time to reignite that inner fire, feel better immediately, and show the world what you're truly capable of.

A note before you begin: As you progress through the seven days, you'll see that some of the instructions are repeated from the previous day and that new instructions are introduced on each successive day.

I structured this 7-day plan this way to build you up gradually and not overload you all at once. Bottom line, it's all about making this work for YOU.

Take this seriously and you'll experience serious results — *FAST.*

Day 1: Reflection and Goal-Setting

- Wake up, turn off all devices, or put them in airplane mode.
- Pour yourself a liter of room temperature water and squeeze one-fourth to half a lemon into it, adding a pinch of pink Himalayan salt, (about one teaspoon).
- Drink the water.
- Go for a quick walk or do one of the simple movement routines found here: https://www.acceleratedmethod.com/movement
- End your morning routine with a contrast shower, (30-sec warm water, 10-sec cold water, and gradually increase the time you're in cold water over time).
- Reflect on your "why" and write down your motivations. Ask yourself questions such as, "What benefits will I gain by improving my health?", "What

are the specific areas of my life that will improve?", and "How will I feel when I am healthier?" Take some time to really reflect on these questions and write down your answers.

Example: *"I want to improve my health so that I can have more energy and feel better about myself. I want to be able to play with my kids without feeling exhausted all the time. I want to be able to fit into my clothes better and feel more confident in my appearance."*

- Set achievable and realistic goals. Write down what you want to achieve and what specific steps you will take to get there. It's important to make your goals specific and measurable so that you can track your progress and stay motivated.

  Example: *"I want to lose 5 pounds in the next month. I will achieve this by exercising for at least 20 to 24 minutes a day, at least 4 days a week, and by eating a balanced diet with fewer processed foods, lean protein, healthy fats, and more vegetables."*

- Take small, practical steps toward your goals. Break down your goals into smaller, more achievable steps so that you don't feel overwhelmed. Focus on making small changes that you can maintain over time.

  Example: *"Instead of trying to overhaul my entire diet all at once, I will start by replacing my afternoon snack with a healthy protein snack. I will also start going for a 10-minute walk after lunch each day."*

- Start keeping a food diary to monitor daily calorie, protein, fat, and carbohydrate intake.
- Stop consuming caffeine or other stimulants by 1 p.m.
- Have your last big meal of the day at least three hours before bedtime.
- Avoid alcohol three hours before bedtime.
- Turn off work and do a "brain dump," (meaning, in a notebook or on a blank piece of paper, write out all your thoughts, tasks and unfinished to-dos that are circling through your brain at least two hours before bedtime).

Days 2-3: Focus on Nutrition, Movement & Sleep

- Repeat the morning routine from Day 1.
- Incorporate a 15-minute bodyweight resistance movement routine like the ones I've provided here: *https://www.acceleratedmethod.com/movement*
- Replace processed, sugary foods with nutrient-dense alternatives like fruit, nuts, and lean protein.
- Increase your intake of fibrous vegetables like broccoli, cucumbers, spinach, and peppers.
- Optimize your carbohydrate intake by following the Daily Progression Method (in Chapter 8) or saving carbs for later in the day.

- Plan a healthy meal plan for the next 7 days, taking into account personal preferences and dietary restrictions.
- Follow the 90/10 rule, aiming to hit your weekly nutrition goals 90 percent of the time.
- Stop consuming caffeine or other stimulants by 1 p.m.
- Have your last big meal of the day at least 3 hours before bedtime.
- Avoid alcohol 3 hours before bedtime.
- Turn off work and do a brain dump 2 hours before bedtime.
- Gradually establish a bedtime routine, such as reading a non-stimulating book, stretching, or taking a warm shower to signal to the brain that it's time to sleep.
- Avoid screens (TV, phone, and tablet) at least an hour before bedtime.
- Keep the bedroom cool, dark, and quiet.

Days 4-5: Optimize Eating Habits and Physical Activity

- Repeat the morning routine from Day 1 and add the additional movement suggestion in the next step.
- Increase the time on your morning movement

resistance training from 15 minutes to 18 minutes and consider adding dumbbells to your routine similar to the version found in Chapter 9 or over here: *https://www.acceleratedmethod.com/movement*

- Start time-restricted eating by choosing a method that works for you, such as overnight fasting, the 14-hour fast, or the 16/8 method shared in Chapter 8.
- Gradually increase your fasting window each day and track your progress.
- Aim to eat 2-3 meals in the hours after your fast consisting of high protein, healthy fats, and fibrous veggies.
- Consume one more liter of water throughout the day in addition to the liter of water you had in the morning routine.
- Stop consuming caffeine or other stimulants by 1 p.m.
- Have your last big meal of the day at least 3 hours before bedtime.
- Avoid alcohol 3 hours before bedtime.
- Turn off work and do a brain dump 2 hours before bedtime.
- Reduce or eliminate alcoholic beverages from your evening ritual.
- Repeat the bedtime routine from Days 2 and 3.

Days 6-7: Maximize Energy, Mental Clarity, and Focus

- Repeat the morning routine from Day 1.
- Wait 1-2 hours before consuming caffeine in the morning and limit your dose to 100-200 mg, spread strategically,(50 to 100 mg at a single time), throughout the morning.
- Consider incorporating L-Theanine into a morning caffeinated beverage to improve focus without jitters.
- Continue to eat in a time-restricted window. (Either choose the method that worked best for you from Days 4 and 5 or see if you can increase your fasting window a little bit more than the previous days.)
- After your fast, focus on consuming foods high in citicoline like eggs, fish, lean beef, and vegetables, (such as spinach, broccoli, and brussels sprouts).
- Consume 2 more liters of water throughout the day in addition to the liter of water you had in the morning routine.
- Stop consuming caffeine or other stimulants by 1 p.m.
- Have your last big meal of the day at least 3 hours before bedtime.
- Turn off work and do a brain dump 2 hours before bedtime.

- Eliminate any alcoholic beverages from your daily or evening ritual for these final two days.
- Repeat the bedtime routine from Days 2 and 3.

Throughout the week:

- Track your progress. Keep a journal to track your meals, physical activity, and any other relevant information and/or habits that will help achieve your goals.
- Celebrate the progress you've made, the habits you've begun to establish, and make any necessary adjustments to your plan to continue on the path towards improving your overall health.
- Find an accountability partner to keep you focused on your goals such as a mentor, coach, or trusted friend.
- Communicate your goals with family, friends, and colleagues, and ask for their support.
- Take time to plan your schedule before starting your journey to personal growth and fulfillment.

So, there you have it! This 7-day kickstart plan will serve as a catalyst to reignite the energy, drive, and passion you once had in your younger years. All you have to do is, well, *do it.*

It works! And you'll notice significant improvements immediately when you implement this proven framework to kickstart your journey and regain control of your physical and mental well-being. By taking accountability for your actions and setting realistic goals, you'll be well on your way to rediscovering the fire within.

So don't wait any longer, let this initial plan be the spark that ignites your journey to personal growth and fulfillment.

Would You Like Even More Help?

If you'd like my input on how to customize this 7-day plan for yourself... or if you'd like to get some help on how to turn this entire book into a system that works for YOU and your specific situation, then I'd love to help you implement this plan for even better results.

You'll not only get the experience I've gained by applying this system successfully for myself, as well as the hundreds of clients just like yourself, but you'll also get the 1-on-1 accountability that often spells the difference between success and failure.

Click below for an informative, no-pressure chat now, and I look forward to speaking with you.

https://www.acceleratedmethod.com/call

CASE STUDY

Tandy B., Oklahoma, Business Consultant

"I've got more time in the day now. And the list just goes on and on about how much better I feel physically."

"So I knew something was continuing to trend in the wrong direction. My irritability was pretty high, and the people closest to me and my family, my tight team members, they were the ones catching the brunt of this irritation. And just the intensity of frustration and irritation, there's a lot of words we use around that, but I just didn't feel like myself for one thing.

I was just not happy with the way I felt and the way I was starting to feel physically or in my midsection. I was in my mid-40s. And I was not happy.

I was having conversations with my inner circle about how I had to start making some changes. Because what I don't want is to be another 20 years down the road and have mobility problems, heart disease, and diabetes and blood sugar problems- and all those kinds of things that have either been family history, or things I've seen friends and mentors go through.

And I had a heart-to-heart with myself — was I was going to slough off? Or is this an opportunity for me to dig in a little deeper and take action on my rhetoric and what I had been talking about wanting to do better and be better?

I've been able to bring that boiling point way down, and be less reactive. I don't have some of those blood pressure headaches I used to get, I've got more time in my day now, and giving time has created more time. And that's a big deal.

Establishing the structure in the plan was easy to implement. If we want to talk about the physical aspects, I was wearing a 38 pant that I was filling out, and nine weeks later I've got a pair of 34 shorts on, and they're comfortable. I was definitely an extra-large shirt guy. I'm wearing only a large today and feeling much better about things. My gut is not overhanging my belt for the first time in years. I mean, the list just goes on and on about how much better I feel physically."

— Tandy B., Oklahoma, Business Consultant

WHAT TO DO NEXT?

You've reached the finish line (of this book), but your journey to regain your edge has barely begun.

This is the moment you decide what happens next in your life.

Hopefully, reading this book has changed any thoughts of, "I'm sick and tired of being sick and tired" to: "Wow! I now know exactly what I need to do!"

(Translation: "I now have the blueprint to get "back on fire ... in all areas of my life.")

Here's a brief recap of what you've learned:

- We started by showing you that going from sick and tired to back on fire does NOT depend on starving yourself or going beast mode at the gym. (*Whew!*)
- You learned that the six common roadblocks for high-performers over 40 are time, energy, expectations, food, past experience, and stress. And I showed you how to assess each area and make the necessary adjustments.
- You discovered the concept of Health Debt, (what your inaction is actually costing you in measurable

dollars), and why it's the simple actions that are so important and easily overlooked.

- I identified the hidden truths that may have kept you stuck for way too long. For instance, how hormones and inflammation play a huge role in whether or not you are able to hit your goals.
- You should now understand The Oxygen Mask Protocol. You've given so much to the other areas of your life — it's now time to prioritize yourself so you can accomplish your goals and be the man you want to be.
- I explained the surprising (and alarming) science of sleep (Chapter 7).
- You learned how to maximize your performance by unlocking the power of proper nutrition.
- I shared movement and training secrets to help you achieve peak health, defy aging, and ditch the "dad bod" forever.
- You discovered the next level of unlocking your full potential by harnessing the power of mental edge enhancers and why alcohol is the insidious menace hiding in plain sight.
- I showed you how to put an end to the "start-stop" cycle and master the art of consistency.
- You learned that the secret to hitting your goals has nothing to do with your vision board and everything to do with bridging your own mental gap.

- I gave you the three essential steps needed to claim your first win.
- Finally, I gave you a 7-day plan to use as a catalyst to reignite the fire within and transform you from "sick and tired" to "back on fire."

Now it's up to you. I know you have probably tried many different ways to "get better." And I know that, despite your best intentions, those other ways have done very little and only added utter frustration.

Here's what I want you to know: **What you want is within reach**. I mean that 100 percent, period, full stop.

The best version of yourself is achievable. You *can* get there without completely disrupting your already busy life. The goal here is to help you get your life back, not make it harder.

The journey won't be easy- change never is. But if you set yourself up to succeed, fully commit to yourself and your family, as well as surround yourself with the right people to cheer you on, then you can do this!

The first step is the hardest.

Let me help you on your journey to get back on fire.

If you'd like our help on executing this in the fastest manner possible with an accountability process that's proven to work, then click here:

https://www.acceleratedmethod.com/call

Remember to pick up your bonuses!

Bonus #1:
From Sick & Tired to Back On Fire Audiobook

Bonus #2:
"The Winner's Lifestyle - How High Performers Achieve What They Want in Health, Wealth, And Life" (Mini-Course)

Bonus #3:
"Get Your Head In The Game - Clear Out The Mental Clutter and Amplify Your Productivity" (Workshop)

Please visit
https://www.backonfirebook.com/bonuses
to receive them all.

ABOUT THE AUTHOR

Logan Henry was born in Tennessee, but he spent most of his younger years in the Midwest until settling in Charleston, South Carolina — calling it home for nearly 24 years.

Naturally an old soul, Logan has dedicated himself to coaching busy and successful businessmen, as well as high performers in all fields. His focus is on helping these men achieve their goals and reach their full potential. Logan has had his own wellness journey, and he too can relate to a time where the repetition of poor health choices took its toll.

Deciding to put an end to low energy, being out of shape and lacking confidence, Logan's journey would not only change the trajectory of his own life, but he would go on to share his powerful story and insights with men around him who needed it the most.

It didn't come easy, however. Simply knowing where to start was a challenge and he soon felt a bit lost. That's when he found his coach and mentor Greg, a West Point graduate and Army Ranger, who would also go on to make a name for himself in the fitness and self-development industry. And so, in 2012, inspired by the strategies to create the change he wished to see, Logan set off to build an unbeatable program.

When Greg passed away suddenly in a tragic accident in 2015, it sparked a fire in Logan to accomplish something extraordinary. And so, in honor of the friend and mentor who had such a profound impact in his life, Logan dedicated himself to helping others find their own strength and to share with as many men as possible the transformational system that continues to fuel everything he does both personally and professionally.

Now, for the past decade, Logan has coached and mentored hundreds of successful high-performing men from various fields, including, but not limited to, business owners, entrepreneurs, real estate professionals, business leaders, consultants, attorneys, actors, engineers, government officials, and corporate executives. Through Logan's proven methods, systems, and personal guidance, they have become better, stronger, more well-rounded versions of themselves, balancing their professional and personal lives in a way they never thought was possible.

Logan has traveled the world, spending countless hours receiving training and mentorship from the best in health and self-improvement. He remains dedicated to honing the ultimate blueprint for quick and sustainable results as it relates to physical and mental performance.

Logan currently lives in Charleston, S.C., with his wife Erica. They are expecting their first child.

Printed in Great Britain
by Amazon

39177013R00198